W9-ASK-324

LIBERALISM

ITS MEANING AND HISTORY

J. SALWYN SCHAPIRO

Professor Emeritus of History
The City College of New York

AN ANVIL ORIGINAL
under the general editorship of
LOUIS L. SNYDER

D. VAN NOSTRAND COMPANY, INC.
PRINCETON, NEW JERSEY
TORONTO LONDON
NEW YORK

To Kathrine

D. VAN NOSTRAND COMPANY, INC.

120 Alexander St., Princeton, New Jersey (*Principal office*)
257 Fourth Avenue, New York 10, New York
25 Hollinger Rd., Toronto 16, Canada
358, Kensington High Street, London, W.14, England

Published simultaneously in Canada by
D. Van Nostrand Company (Canada), Ltd.

Library of Congress Catalog Card No. 58-8609

PRINTED IN THE UNITED STATES OF AMERICA

PREFACE

Liberalism has been a phenomenon of the Western world, and a modern one. It originated in Western Europe during the fifteenth and sixteenth centuries when the modern order of life was displacing feudalism. During the seventeenth and eighteenth centuries it was introduced into North America by settlers from Europe. From faint beginnings liberalism developed to become, according to the English sociologist, L. T. Hobhouse, "an all-penetrating element of the life-structure of the modern world."

This book describes the origin and development of liberalism in the leading countries of the Western world. Throughout its history liberalism has had to struggle for survival. This is no less true today. In the twentieth century its avowed uncompromising enemy everywhere has been the totalitarian dictatorship of fascism and of communism. Therefore, liberalism has need to clarify its ideas and to strengthen its institutions.

Whatever variations the pattern of liberalism assumed in Western countries were the results of historic conditions and of national character. But its fundamental principles have remained everywhere the same.

The purpose of this volume is to provide an understanding of these principles which are necessary to comprehend fully the problems confronting the liberal world, now challenged by communist totalitarianism.

The author wishes to acknowledge his debt to his wife, Kathrine, whose aid was indispensable in writing this book; and to Mrs. Mary Steg for her proficiency and reliability in typing the manuscript.

January, 1958 J. SALWYN SCHAPIRO

TABLE OF CONTENTS

PART I—LIBERALISM

1. The Meaning of Liberalism 9
2. The Making of the Liberal Mind 14
3. Evolution of Liberalism, Political, Economic, and Social 27
4. Liberalism in Britain: From Laissez Faire to the Welfare State 40
5. Liberalism in France: Progress and Reaction 50
6. Liberalism in Italy: Monarchical and Republican 60
7. Liberalism in Germany: An Unfinished Pattern 68
8. Liberalism in America: From Jeffersonian Democracy to the New Deal 77
9. The Lasting Values of Liberalism 89

PART II—READINGS

1. HOBHOUSE: Liberalism and the Individual 93
2. SOCRATES: Intellectual Freedom 94
3. ABÉLARD: Yea and Nay 96
4. ERASMUS: The Philosophy of Christ 98
5. DESCARTES: The Methods of Reasoning 100
6. MILTON: Censorship 101
7. CONDORCET: The Meaning of Progress 103
8. LOCKE: Religion, No Concern of the Government 105
9. VOLTAIRE: Reason and Tolerance 107
10. CONDORCET: A National System of Education 109
11. SMITH: Advantages of Free Enterprise 112
12. LOCKE: Government by the Consent of the Governed 115
13. MONTESQUIEU: Separation of the Powers of Government 118
14. ROUSSEAU: Interpretation of the Social Contract 120
15. The English Bill of Rights 122

16. Declaration of Independence 124
17. The American Bill of Rights 126
18. The Declaration of the Rights of Man and of the Citizen 128
19. RICARDO: On Labor, and on Free Trade 131
20. MALTHUS: Subsistence and Population 133
21. SPENCER: Survival of the Economically Fit 136
22. DEWEY: Individualism Under a Socialized Economy 138
23. Universal Declaration of Human Rights 139
24. BENTHAM: The Principle of Utility 143
25. COBDEN: Free Trade and Universal Peace 144
26. MILL: Necessity of Working Class Representation 145
27. MILL: Freedom of Individual Opinion 146
28. The People's Charter 149
29. HOBHOUSE: State Intervention 151
30. Aims of the British Labor Party 152
31. BEVERIDGE: Social Security as a Duty of the State 153
32. GUIZOT: The Bourgeoisie, Upholder of Freedom 155
33. GUIZOT: Property and the Expansion of the Suffrage 157
34. TOCQUEVILLE: Development of the Principle of Equality 158
35. GAMBETTA: Democracy and Freedom 160
36. The Saint-Mandé Program 162
37. MAZZINI: Nationalism and Democracy 164
38. HEGEL: The State as the Divine Idea 166
39. The Fundamental Rights of the German People 168
40. TROELTSCH: The German View of Freedom 171
41. TREITSCHKE: The State as Power 172
42. BISMARCK: State Intervention to Protect the Workers 174
43. The Northwest Ordinance of 1787 175
44. JEFFERSON: Toleration of Political Differences 177
45. LINCOLN: The Meaning of Equality 178
46. LINCOLN: The Gettysburg Address 180
47. The Civil War Amendments to the Constitution 181
48. BRANDEIS: Political Liberty and Industrial Absolutism 182

49. Franklin D. Roosevelt: A New Bill of Rights 184
50. Decision of the Supreme Court Against Segregation in Public Schools 185
A Select Bibliography 187
Index 189
List of Anvil Books 192

Part I

LIBERALISM

— 1 —

THE MEANING OF LIBERALISM

Origin of "Liberalism." The term "liberalism" is as modern as its meaning. It is Spanish in origin, from the name of a political party, the "Liberales" that early in the nineteenth century advocated constitutional government for Spain. Later "liberal" was a term taken over in other countries to designate a government, a party, a policy, an opinion that favored freedom as opposed to authoritarianism. As a philosophy liberalism does not fall into the category of a closed system of thought, with fixed, unchanging dogmas. Rather may it be characterized as an attitude of mind toward life and life's problems that stresses the values of freedom for individuals, for minorities, and for nations.

Liberalism, the Way of Freedom. What has characterized liberalism at all times is its unshaken belief in the necessity of freedom to achieve every desirable aim. A deep concern for the freedom of the individual inspired its opposition to absolute authority, be it that of the state, of the church, or of a political party. The fundamental postulate of liberalism has been the moral worth, the absolute value, and the essential dignity of the human personality. Every individual is therefore to be treated as an end in himself, not as a means to advance the interests of others. The political liberty of the individual consists, according to the French Declaration of the Rights of Man, "in the power of doing whatever does not injure another . . . limits are determinable only by law." Liberals are deeply convinced that without liberty life is not worth living. Hence, they have ever sought to free the individual from unjust and hampering restraints imposed upon him by governments, institutions, and traditions. An autonomous individual would be free to choose his occupation, to assert his opinions, to change his nationality, and to move from place to place. Liberalism, according to L. T. Hobhouse, "is the belief that society can safely be founded on this self-directing power of personality." (*See Reading No. 1.*)

Closely linked to the freedom of the individual is that of association. Liberalism has advocated the right to form associations of all kinds—political, social, economic, religious, and cultural—that have as their objective the advancement of the legitimate interests of their members. Without freedom of association the individual would be helpless in opposing the restraints imposed by the established order. With it the power of numbers, arising from a cohesive group of like-minded individuals, can be asserted against injustice and tyranny.

Liberalism and Equal Rights. Equality is another fundamental liberal principle. Liberalism has proclaimed the principle of equality for all human beings everywhere. It must be borne in mind, however, that equality does not mean that all have equal ability, or equal moral perception, or equal personal attraction. What it means is that all have equal rights before the law, and that all are entitled to civil liberty. No law should confer special privileges on some, and impose special discriminations on others; it must be the same for all whether it aids, protects, or punishes. Liberalism has waged unceasing war against privilege, whether that of birth, wealth, race, creed, or sex, as an artificial hindrance to individual development. As liberalism progressed, the principle of equality was extended to include universal, equal suffrage. In our day liberalism is aiming to establish a society in which there would be equal opportunity for all to make the most of their natural endowments, be these great or small.

Liberalism and Government. The main impact of liberalism has been on government, as the institution with supreme power in the community. In the liberal view the chief end of government is to uphold the liberty, equality, and security of all citizens. For this reason, a liberal government, whether in form monarchical or republican, rests on the rule of law emanating from a law-making body freely elected by the people. No government is, therefore, legitimate, according to liberalism, unless it is based on the consent of the governed. In order to protect the rights of individuals and of minorities, liberalism has placed highly important limitations on the power of government. These rights, known variously as "civil liberties," "natural rights," and the "rights of man," consist, according to the American Declaration of Independence, of "life, liberty and the pursuit of happiness," and according to the French Declaration of the Rights of Man, of "liberty, property, security, and resistance of oppression." They are inviolable, inalienable, and universal. All acts of the government in relation to the individual citizen must be according to due process of law, the violation of which is halted by an independent judiciary. The liberal state is not the god-state of the Roman emperors, or the absolute state of the divine right monarchs, or the garrison state of the military dictators, or the totalitarian state of the communists and fascists. It is a government of laws, not of men.

Liberalism and Intellectual Freedom. Of all civil liberties, the most prized has been liberty of thought and expression. Liberals came to the deep conviction that all opinions, even erroneous ones, should have freedom of expression. Not infrequently have opinions, commonly held to be false, proved to be true. Furthermore, in the conflict between opinions even error serves a useful purpose in that it stimulates truth to clarify and fortify itself. For these reasons liberals have been in the forefront of movements to abolish censorships, whether official or non-official, as the chief hindrances to the peaceful progress of mankind. The case for intellectual freedom was well stated by Justice Oliver Wendell Holmes when he declared that "the ultimate good desired is better reached by free trade in ideas—that the best test of truth is the power of thought to get itself accepted in the competition of the market, and that truth is the only ground upon which their wishes safely can be carried out."

Liberalism and Rationalism. The stress placed by liberalism on intellectual freedom derives from the conviction that man is essentially a rational creature—not indeed that he is always reasonable, but that he has the faculty of being so. Liberals in general have believed in the existence of objective truth, discoverable through reason according to the scientific method of research, experiment, and verification. What is known as rationalism endeavors, by using reason, to subject all matters, religious as well as non-religious, to critical inquiry. The rationalist looks primarily to science for enlightenment. Reason, not revelation, is his mentor. Hence, what cannot stand the test of reason is not to be accepted, no matter how great the authority behind it.

Liberalism and Religion. In general, liberals have been rationalists. As a consequence they have developed what may be called a secular attitude toward religion. In their view, a religion is an opinion to be tolerated like all other opinions; and a church is a private institution to be accepted like all other institutions. Liberalism has advocated freedom of non-belief as well as of belief. To achieve complete religious freedom required the secularization of public life. Everywhere, liberals generally have advocated separation of church and state; secular, public education; civil marriage; and laws permitting divorce.

Liberalism and Progress. Because of its secular attitude liberalism adopted a dynamic view of life, envisaging progress for mankind. It has therefore exerted every effort to make this world a better place in which to live. Man, according to liberalism, is born ignorant, not wicked; and throughout his life he is conditioned by a social environment that in many ways has been the product of the errors and injustices of the past. To rectify this situation it is necessary, therefore, to increase the sum of knowledge, to strive for enlightenment, and to create a society that will promote peace, prosperity, and good will. These views of the nature of man and of society were derived from the idea of progress, an idea both modern and characteristically liberal. Vaguely conceived in the seventeenth century, boldly proclaimed in the eighteenth, the idea of progress became an article of faith in the nineteenth. According to the liberal view progress, slow at one time and rapid at another, results in transforming one system of society which is bad but not too bad, to another which is good but not too good. Always has mankind been advancing, steadily, continually, and inevitably to an ever better civilization, a process that will go on indefinitely. Only by his own efforts can man create for himself a better life on earth. Belief in progress has inspired liberals to become the ardent advocates of reforms of all kinds in order to create the good society of the future. Reform has been the passion of liberalism.

Way of Liberalism. The liberal temper blends idealism with practical considerations. Ideals are to serve as guides to ultimate ends. These are to be attained, not all at once but one by one, cautiously, moderately, yet continuously. Hence, the liberal is neither a romantic dreaming of an imaginary past wherein all was idyllic; nor is he a utopian dreaming of an imaginary future when a perfect society will be established once for all. Time, place, and history determine the pace as well as the method of progress. The liberal way is the way of the "inevitability of gradualness" in the progress of mankind.

— 2 —

THE MAKING OF THE LIBERAL MIND

Socrates. Liberalism as an attitude toward life—skeptical, experimental, rational, free—was given expression by extraordinary individuals long before the Modern Age. A notable liberal in ancient times was Socrates (c. 470-399 B.C.), whose life and death bore eloquent testimony to his belief in freedom of inquiry and of expression. Virtue, he contended, comes from knowledge; and knowledge, from an insistent examination of one's beliefs. An unexamined life, he asserted, is not worth living. When condemned to death on the charge of corrupting the youth of Athens, Socrates made the following declaration, "I say . . . either acquit me, or do not acquit me: but be sure that I shall not alter my way of life; no, not if I have to die for it many times." (*See Reading No. 2.*)

Abélard. In medieval times another liberal voice was heard, that of Peter Abélard (1079-1142). He was a theologian who refused to accept unquestioningly the authority of the Church Fathers. The master key of knowledge, according to Abélard, is a persistent and frequent questioning. In his book, *Sic et Non* (*Yea and Nay*) he propounded a number of theological problems such as, "Is God one or no?," and "Is God a substance or no?" In treating each he balances arguments, pro and con, citing authorities, but draws no definite conclusion. (*See Reading No. 3.*) By emphasizing the power of reason, Abélard's method introduced an element of doubt, thereby opening the way to independent thinking.

Modern Liberals. At the dawn of the Modern Age appeared a number of pioneers of the liberal way of thinking. The most notable were the Netherlander, Desiderius Erasmus (1465-1536); the Frenchman, René Descartes (1596-1650); and the Englishman, John Milton (1608-1674).

Erasmus, the outstanding Christian humanist of the Renaissance, taught that the ideals of humanism could find a place within the Christian faith. He was deeply convinced that the true Christian had nothing to fear from the advance of knowledge, whether in philosophy, in science, or in history, as nothing could possibly invalidate the teachings of Christ "the philosopher," the truest and noblest ever known. (*See Reading No. 4.*) His free-ranging spirit and sweet reasonableness caused this Christian humanist to turn away from the rigid scholasticism of the theologians as he did from the vituperative violence of Martin Luther. Erasmus "stepped quietly from the medieval to the modern world."

What has been called a revolution in the ways of thinking was effected by Descartes. In clear, simple language his book, *Discourse on Method,* boldly proclaimed the sovereignty of reason in human affairs. Reason, and only reason, was, according to Descartes, the sole method of discovering truth. Only those ideas were true, he declared, that were "presented to my mind so clearly and distinctly as to exclude all ground of doubt." All ideas were to be subjected to the process of rational thought. (*See Reading No. 5.*) Descartes proclaimed supreme confidence in the human mind, the independence of which was not to be limited by authority, no matter how ancient and how revered. And all men everywhere were endowed with reason, even though it might be undeveloped. Hence, his famous maxim, "I think, therefore I am," which he accepted as the first principle of his philosophy. Descartes was the father of what became known as rationalism, the basic idea of the eighteenth century Enlightenment.

Unhindered freedom to publish found an early champion in Milton. His pamphlet, *Areopagitica,* is a classic document in the history of intellectual freedom. It was issued as a protest against the establishment by parliament of a board of censors with power to issue or withhold licenses to publish. In words of ringing eloquence,

Milton denounced censorship as a destroyer of the life of the mind. Books, he declared, were live things; hence, to destroy a book by forbidding its publication was to destroy living thought. (*See Reading No. 6.*) Milton's pleas for freedom of publication became powerful weapons used by English liberals in the movement to abolish censorship.

Beginnings of Liberalism. These pioneers of liberalism were voices crying in a wilderness. As a *movement,* liberalism had its early beginnings in the Renaissance, in the Protestant Reformation, and in the Scientific Revolution. The spirit of the Renaissance was secular, which had the effect of shifting human interest from the next world to life upon earth. Through its fundamental doctrine of private judgment in interpreting the Bible, Protestantism promoted individualism in religion. As a consequence, a diversity of Christian sects took the place of the one, authoritative Catholic church. Closely related to the rise of liberalism was the scientific revolution of the sixteenth and seventeenth centuries. It revealed the world to be a machine run by universal, automatic, immutable laws that operated smoothly and infallibly. The scientific method of discovering truth became the model for liberalism.

The Enlightenment. As a system of thought, liberalism may be said to have received definite expression during the eighteenth century. This period, known as the Enlightenment and as the Age of Reason, witnessed an intellectual revolution that spread to almost every land of the Western World. Famous thinkers appeared whose influence profoundly changed the ideas and attitudes of their age. Most notable were Voltaire, Rousseau, Diderot, and Montesquieu in France; Locke, Hume, and Adam Smith in Britain; Goethe, Lessing, and Kant in Germany; Vico and Beccaria in Italy; and Jefferson, Franklin, and Paine in America. Their views comprehended a system of political, social, economic, and cultural philosophy that, in the nineteenth century, received the name "liberalism."

The liberal mind was now in the making. What ingredients were put into it? What forms did it take? What methods did it use? Answers to these questions were most effectively given in France, which became the head and center of the Enlightenment. There, a school of thinkers arose, known as the philosophes, the most notable of whom were those already mentioned. The philosophes repudiated the institutions, ideas, and traditions of the Old Regime, as the system prior to the French Revolution was known. They developed a new pattern of life and thought in books of great originality and of unmatched literary power. As a consequence, this pattern became, to a more or less degree, the model for liberal thinkers everywhere.

(1) **Nature.** Fundamental in this pattern was the role of nature in the affairs of man. A rediscovery of nature took place, and men beheld a world governed beneficently by impersonal natural laws. The natural order served as a model for the establishment of new systems of government and society, even of morality and religion. The nearer a new system approached what was regarded as the model of nature, the nearer it was to perfection. Nature was held aloft as the prime source of justice, of virtue, and of beneficence.

Natural law, an old idea, was given a new significance in the eighteenth century. It was made the acid test of the legitimacy of the existing order of government and society. If an institution worked badly because of privileges, prejudice, and tyranny it was regarded as artificial. Hence, it was to be abolished, and a new, enlightened one established based on natural law. In human affairs, as in those of nature, there existed natural laws that could be discovered by the scientific method of investigation.

(2) **Reason.** Reason, not faith as formerly, was regarded as the only true instrument to guide man on his new voyage of discovery. The thinkers of the Enlightenment were convinced that reason was less a possession than a process of acquisition, "a sort of energy, a force, a means by which to do something," according to Arthur M. Wilson's *Diderot: The Testing Years, 1713-1759.* The "ferment of universal reason" united all peoples into a common humanity. Only by using reason could man comprehend and solve the problems that faced him. If given free play and full expression reason would create a new system of living that would bring happiness to man in this world.

(3) **Goodness of Man.** Man was also naturally inclined to be good, unless corrupted by ignorance and prejudice. This dictum of the philosophers of the Enlightenment was contrary to the Christian belief in original sin. Man's natural goodness was eloquently proclaimed by Jean-Jacques Rousseau. He developed a theory that man in the state of nature was possessed of goodness which degenerated into corruption as a result of the coming of civilization. The existing social order was therefore the heritage of an evil past created by ignorance, violence, and tyranny. What was essential, according to Rousseau, was to establish a natural social order, one in harmony with man's goodness. Only then will the problems arising from the conflict between man and society be solved.

(4) **Progress.** The new faith in man and the new passion for change were inspired by the idea of progress. By progress was meant that man has moved, is moving, and will move in a beneficial direction. To the philosophers of the Enlightenment this idea was the driving force of man's ceaseless efforts to create for himself a happy future. Progress is the leading theme of Marquis de Condorcet's book, *Sketch for a Historical Picture of the Progress of the Human Mind.* According to Condorcet, progress is an autonomous, linear, inevitable historical movement toward "perfectibility," the golden age of the future. Changes for the better come as a result of new discoveries in the arts and sciences, and of greater enlightenment in moral ideas and practices. (*See Reading No. 7.*) The mortal enemies of progress have been fanaticism, dogmatism, and unreasonableness. In his book, a monument of liberal thought, Condorcet presents a great vision of the future of mankind. He foretells a system of life in which would exist equality between nations; equality between individuals within a nation; equality between the sexes; the abolition of war, poverty, slavery, and colonialism; the establishment of universal literacy; and an increase in man's longevity. With the idea of progress came a new vista of man's "perfectibility" and future happiness.

(5) **Secularism.** Belief in the idea of progress promoted a this-worldly attitude of mind known as secularism. In its militant aspect the secularism of the Enlightenment warred against all revealed religions as having their origin

in the fears and superstitions of primitive life. The "broad river of incredulity" which flowed through the eighteenth century loosened the foundations of faith in traditional religion. According to secularism, man's supreme aim was to attain happiness in this world through mundane ideas and scientific methods. Most of the thinkers of the Enlightenment believed in deism, or natural religion, according to which God created the world and the natural laws that governed it. But they disbelieved in theological dogmas, flouted rituals, and repudiated churches. Especially did they oppose the intervention of churches in the affairs of government. A "solid wall" was to be erected between church and state by making religion a private matter.

Secularism in the field of morality found its greatest exponent in the German philosopher, Immanuel Kant (1724-1804). His work, *Critique of Pure Reason* created what has been called the idealist system of philosophy.

According to Kant, an invisible, an "ideal," world exists, ruled by moral laws as universal as the natural laws that rule the physical world. The inhabitant of this ideal world, man, is by his very nature a moral being. The idea of right being implanted in every individual, conscience reveals to him what is right and wrong. From this arises what Kant called the Categorical Imperative, the absolute moral law of rational, self-determining beings. It is formulated as follows. "So act, that the rule on which you act admits of being adopted as a law by all rational beings." The Categorical Imperative is not imposed from the outside by a deity; hence man has no need of supernatural guidance. Kant repudiated all forms of revealed religion, which he regarded as no longer necessary to man's moral progress.

(6) **Toleration.** A pioneer of toleration was the Englishman, John Locke (1632-1704). In his *Letter Concerning Toleration* he argued that the power of civil government is limited to matters of this world, and has nothing to do with the world of the hereafter. A church, he defined as "a voluntary society of men" dedicated "to the public worshipping of God." Therefore, its power to punish should be limited to the ousting of refractory members. Religious views should not be imposed on any-

one; neither should the laws forbid the profession of any faith whatsoever. However, Locke did not extend toleration to Catholics and atheists. (*See Reading No. 8.*)

The great apostle of religious toleration in the eighteenth century was François Marie Arouet de Voltaire (1694-1778). In his *Treatise on Tolerance* he ridiculed the prevailing idea that toleration would disturb domestic tranquility. With great wit and eloquence he pleaded for freedom of all kinds of belief and disbelief. Such freedom, he argued, would strengthen the power of reason to destroy fanaticism and to stop persecution. To Voltaire, religious intolerance was not only evil but also ridiculous. (*See Reading No. 9.*) Toleration, he argued, would inspire loyalty to the state in citizens of different faiths, and friendly relations between Catholic and Protestant nations.

(7) **Intellectual Freedom.** Religious toleration was part of the general movement for intellectual freedom. In almost every country of Western Europe there existed formidable censorships of printed matter, established by the government and the church, that seriously hindered intellectual freedom. If there was one thing on which the thinkers of the Enlightenment were agreed it was "freedom of thought and expression." This became their battle cry. They were convinced that once this freedom was established, the problems of the world would in time be solved peacefully and equitably.

In the war against censorship the greatest battle was fought and won by Denis Diderot as editor of the French *Encyclopedia* during the period of its publication, 1751-1765. This famous encyclopedia was the collective work of many thinkers who contributed articles attacking the evils of the day: religious fanaticism, feudalism, arbitrary government, restrictions on commerce, censorship, and suppression of personal liberty. The work was condemned by the government, by the church, and even by the Sorbonne. Diderot, by using all sorts of stratagems to defy the censorship, finally succeeded in having the entire *Encyclopedia* published. This greatest single work of the Enlightenment became a powerful weapon, used by the French philosophes, to destroy the Old Regime.

(8) **Education.** Inevitably those who sought to create the liberal mind became interested in education.

In this, as in other fields, they were inspired by that fountainhead of liberal thought, Locke. His "sensation" theory may be described as the starting point of modern education. According to Locke, a child comes into the world with its mind a "blank page"; knowledge is acquired as a result of impressions, "sensations," received from the environment outside. Therefore, the school is the most important of all institutions in shaping the human mind. The liberal educators of the Enlightenment were convinced that by giving a new content to education, by devising new methods, and especially by spreading it to all the people the school would become the chief instrument of progress. A nation could not be free and ignorant.

The new education had advocates in many parts of the Western world. Chief among them was Jean-Jacques Rousseau (1712-1778), whose famous book, *Émile,* has been considered the Magna Charta of modern education. Rousseau proclaimed the idea that in teaching the young, both content and method should be in harmony with the nature of the child and of the world in which it lives. Another pioneer of popular education was Thomas Jefferson, who advocated the creation of a system of elementary education, public, free and secular. "If a nation expects to be ignorant and free, in a state of civilization," he declared, "it expects what never was and never will be." Popular education would become an instrument for the amelioration of the condition of the poor, and for the encouragement of the "mass of talents which lies buried in every country."

The most advanced educational ideas of the eighteenth century were propounded by Marquis de Condorcet (1743-1794). In his "Report to the Legislative Assembly" (1792), Condorcet recommended the establishment in France of a national system of education, from the lowest to the highest grade, that would be free, universal, and secular. Teaching in this system was to be motived by the libertarian ideas of the French Revolution. (*See Reading No. 10.*)

(9) **Economics.** No important aspect of human life was left out of the pattern of liberalism created by the Enlightenment. As environment was considered all im-

portant in this pattern, considerable attention was devoted to the study of economics. The pioneers of economic liberalism were the Physiocrats, a group of French thinkers the most important of whom was François Quesnay (1694-1774). The Physiocrats were convinced that natural laws governed the production and distribution of wealth. To them the only true source of wealth was agriculture, which they asserted alone produced a surplus above what was expended in the production of a crop. Economic laws were the only true natural laws in the field of human relations; all other laws were artificial; hence, limited in scope. Obedience to natural economic laws would bring riches, and disobedience, poverty. Such activities as buying and selling, producing and consuming were to be free, unhampered by regulations imposed by governments. The famous expression, "laissez faire" was coined by a Physiocrat. It meant that governments were to keep their hands off the economic activities of individuals in order to give free scope to the working of the natural economic laws. Another significant aspect of Physiocratic economics was the emphasis placed on the role of capital in production.

If the science of economics can be said to have had a father he was the Scotsman, Adam Smith (1723-1790). His book, *Wealth of Nations* (1776), became the great source of the ideas and policies distinctive of economic liberalism. Adam Smith took much from the Physiocrats but not their leading idea that agriculture was the sole source of the wealth produced. In his view commerce and industry, as well as agriculture, were productive of wealth.

How to increase the wealth of a nation? Adam Smith gave his answer which if followed would promote national prosperity. Everyone, he asserted, has a natural propensity to trade, which if given free rein, would stimulate economic activity resulting in an increase in the production of goods. Every trader is dominated by the profit motive, which inspires his activity. It therefore follows that the enterpriser who acts from selfish motives is, nevertheless, led "by an invisible hand" to promote the general good. In other words, the selfish interest of the enterpriser harmonizes with national prosperity, thereby benefiting all: government, business, and labor.

All important in economic life, therefore, is the role of the businessman. He knows his own interests far better than any government can tell him. Hence, the only wise policy for a government to follow is laissez faire. Adam Smith limited the role of government chiefly to the defense of the nation against foreign aggression, and to the protection of the life, liberty, and property of the citizens. He favored the abolition of the restrictions imposed on commerce and industry by the mercantilist policies of the government. All producers were to be free to compete in a free market: to sell their goods, their services, and their labor at prices determined by competition. In this "obvious and simple system of natural liberty" there would exist freedom of trade between nations, freedom of contract between buyer and seller, freedom of labor, and freedom of enterprise. (*See Reading No. 11.*) So great was the influence of the economic teachings of Adam Smith that it was said of him that he "persuaded his own generation and governed the next."

(10) Government. How was the liberal order, in all its ramifications, to come into existence? Through legislation, was the answer of the thinkers of the Enlightenment. But with the exception of that in Britain, the government of every fairly large European country was virtually an absolute monarchy and a vital part of the old order that was to be abolished. The problem arose of transforming the state from that of being the upholder of the status quo into an instrument for the promotion of progress. In order to solve this problem the political philosophers of the Enlightenment were led to examine and analyze new ideas concerning the state, its origin, its functions, and its powers, in order to find ways and means to utilize it for their purposes

These ideas had their inspiration in the philosophy of John Locke (1632-1704), whose *Of Civil Government* (1690) developed the seminal ideas of political liberalism. According to Locke, the state came into existence as a result of a "social contract" between individuals living independently in a state of nature. The object of the contract was to have a common authority to end the confusion, the uncertainty, and the inconveniences of life under natural conditions. This common authority, the state is, therefore, based on popular consent. It exercises limited powers; the social contract does not abjure the individual's natural rights to life, liberty, and property. What if a government violates these natural rights? Then the people would be justified in overthrowing it through revolution, and in establishing a new government that would respect their natural rights. The justification of revolution to maintain the original social contract was the novel idea advanced by Locke. (*See Reading No. 12.*)

What have been accepted as basic liberal principles of government have in the main been derived from Locke's political philosophy. These principles may be summarized as follows. (a) A government cannot be regarded as "legitimate" unless it is based on the consent of the governed. (b) The natural rights of the citizen are protected against any infraction by arbitrary acts of the government. (c) No power in the state may be exercised without responsibility; hence, periodic popular elections. (d) Finally, revolution is justified whenever a government becomes despotic by violating natural rights or by suppressing popular elections.

Another version of political liberalism was propounded by the Frenchman, Charles Louis de Secondat, Baron de la Brède et de la Montesquieu (1689-1775). He did not accept the theory of the social contract, but sought other ways to preserve political freedom. In his book, *The Spirit of Laws,* he propounded another famous theory, the separation of the powers of government. In Montesquieu's view there exists a natural tendency for those in power to abuse their authority; and whatever the form of government, abuse of power is tyranny. How, then, can such abuse be automatically prevented? Freedom would be maintained, argued Montesquieu, by a system of government in which the executive, legislative, and judicial powers are distinct and separate. Each power would then check and balance the others. Despotism results when the three powers of government are in one hand, whether in that of an individual or of a body. (*See*

Reading No. 13.) The theory of the separation of powers profoundly influenced, in some lands, the making of the liberal state.

A distinctly democratic aspect of the liberal state was the contribution of the French Swiss, Jean-Jacques Rousseau (1712-1778). In his *Social Contract,* Rousseau presented a far more radical version of the social contract theory than that presented by Locke. When forming the state, he contended, every individual surrendered all his rights to the community, which then became sovereign. A new supreme authority in government now appeared, the people. This is the doctrine of popular sovereignty. According to Rousseau, it is absolute, inviolate, inalienable, and indivisible. When the voice of every citizen is heard in the law-making body, the original terms of the social contract are fulfilled. Hence, "obedience to a self-prescribed law is liberty." Under such a system the sovereign power neither has nor can have any interest contrary to that of the people; therefore no need exists for special guarantees of civil rights. A law is legitimate only when it expresses the "general will," or the will of the citizens to advance the common welfare. What if the government acts contrary to the "general will"? Rousseau does not answer directly, but he implies that the people would be justified in overthrowing it. (*See Reading No. 14.*) The great contribution of Rousseau to the making of the liberal state was the doctrine of popular sovereignty as expressed in universal suffrage.

Influence of the Philosophes. Fearless, honest search for truth was the supreme characteristic of the great thinkers of the Enlightenment. They were profoundly convinced that reason was the best instrument with which to seek and to find the truth in any and all fields. Because of their faith in reason they waged unceasing warfare against superstition, obscurantism, and prejudice. In their devoted efforts to reduce social and political problems to scientific terms they formulated universal principles to be applied to concrete problems and situations. Not a little of their success came from graces of style, especially notable in the writings of the French philosophes. The reader was entranced by the compressed clarity and sparkling wit of Voltaire, the poetic eloquence of Rousseau, the serene elegance of Montesquieu, and the scintillating vivaciousness of Diderot. Style gave learning an attraction hardly known heretofore.

The thinkers of the Enlightenment expressed the rising tide of public opinion in almost every Western land. Feudalism, mercantilism, absolute monarchy, and censorship, still widely prevalent on the Continent, felt the impact of the intellectual revolution. The new ideas made an especial appeal to the rising middle class, resentful of the restraints on its economic activities and of the privileges enjoyed by the nobility. The great struggles that followed resulted in making liberalism the accepted pattern of life for the peoples of the Western world.

— 3 —

EVOLUTION OF LIBERALISM, POLITICAL, ECONOMIC, AND SOCIAL

Rise of the Bourgeoisie. The making of the liberal mind during the eighteenth century was not an isolated event. It was closely associated with the rise of the bourgeoisie which, since the Commercial Revolution that followed the discovery of America, had been growing in numbers, wealth, and influence. Its ideals, interests, and ambitions were in direct conflict with those of the authoritarian state of absolute monarchy. To make the changes necessary to create a new order, the bourgeoisie had to become the dominant power in the state. This meant revolution.

Revolution of 1688. Like evolution, revolution is a modern idea. By overthrowing the existing government through a popular uprising a revolution aims to put into the seats of power those committed to the establishment of new institutions and new values. Success is of the essence. If the uprising fails it is termed a rebellion. Many rebellions have taken place in history but comparatively few revolutions, and these have occurred in modern times.

England is the pioneer land of revolution. The English Revolution of 1688 may be described as the first uprising that succeeded in overthrowing a despotic ruler and in establishing, firmly and permanently, a new system of government in which parliament was definitely recognized as the supreme power in the government, a principle basic in political liberalism. The new government took the form of a limited, or constitutional, monarchy, in which the powers of the king were limited to "executive" functions.

Constitutional changes followed the Revolution. The Bill of Rights (1689) guaranteed the privileges of members of Parliament and the rights of Englishmen. (*See Reading No. 15.*) The Toleration Act (1688) granted a fair degree of religious freedom by extending toleration to Dissenters, Protestants who did not belong to the established Anglican church. The Mutiny Act (1689) in effect established the supremacy of the civil over the military power. Liberty of the press was established in 1695 by abolishing the official censorship. These measures constituted important steps in the progress of liberalism.

Party Government. For the first time in history the liberal state appeared, at least in outline form. The system of constitutional government was definitely committed to the maintenance of the "liberty of the subject," or the rights of Englishmen. Political parties, essential to the working of the liberal state, were organized. Party strife at the polls between Tories and Whigs for the control of the government became the political equivalent of civil war. Heads were counted, not broken, in the struggle for the control of the government. Though the size of the electorate was greatly limited by property and other qualifications, and party organization was loose and fluid, government by the majority party now made its historic appearance. From this was derived the distinctively liberal principle, new in the annals of government, namely, the right of opposition. Hitherto, opposition to the government was regarded as treason, and punished as such. Now the minority in parliament had the legal right, even the duty, to oppose the policies of the ruling majority. Periodic popular elections were to determine which party would be the government, and which party the opposition. Power in the government, according to liberal doctrine, rested on responsibility to the electorate.

The American Revolution. The next great advance in creating the liberal state was made by the American Revolution of 1776. The Declaration of Independence asserted for the first time officially that governments derived "their just powers from the consent of the governed." In addition, the Declaration proclaimed "that all men are created equal" with "unalienable Rights" to

"Life, Liberty and the pursuit of Happiness," which could not be rightfully suppressed. It was therefore the right, even the duty, of a people to overthrow a despotic government. (*See Reading No. 16.*)

More firmly and more deeply did the American Revolution lay the foundation of the liberal state, by its emphasis on natural rights and on human equality. Its end product was the Constitution of the United States. Both in its inception and in its provisions the Constitution marked a milestone in the history of political liberalism. It was the first written constitution adopted by a convention chosen specifically for this purpose. It created a federal republic new in design, in scope, and in power. The central principle of the new government, the separation of powers, was designed to prevent tyranny by having the executive, legislative, and judicial powers, checking and balancing each other. By the amendment clause the Constitution provided machinery for peaceful changes in the system of government. Supremacy of the civil over the military power was assured by the provision that no appropriation for the army "shall be for a longer term than two years."

The Bill of Rights, or the first ten amendments, went much further on the road of liberalism than had the English Bill of Rights. It *guaranteed* freedom of religion, speech, press, and assembly. (*See Reading No. 17.*) By forbidding the establishment of a national church it created a precedent for the separation of church and state on the national level. These innovations became an inspiration for liberals the world over.

The French Revolution. Even more advanced in its liberal tenets than the American Revolution was the French Revolution of 1789. According to the Declaration of the Rights of Man, the object of government was the preservation of his natural and inalienable rights to liberty, property, security, and resistance to oppression. The doctrine of popular sovereignty was clearly proclaimed in the statement that the people were the source of all sovereignty; hence, all citizens were to have the right to participate in the making of laws. Equality was greatly stressed. Men were born free and equal, asserted the Declaration, hence they were to be equal before the law, and equally eligible "to all honors, places, and employments," according to their different abilities. (*See Reading No. 18.*)

The French Revolution was both a political and a social revolution. As a political revolution it overthrew absolute monarchy, and established the liberal state by the constitution of 1791, according to which France became a limited monarchy; the executive power was entrusted to the king, and the legislative power, to a unicameral legislature elected by a propertied suffrage. As a social revolution, it destroyed the Old Regime by drastic reforms, the most important of which were the abolition of feudalism, the confiscation of the lands of the emigrant nobles and of the church, and the suppression of the monopolistic guilds and corporations. A new, a liberal social order was created by parceling out the sequestered lands to peasants and bourgeois; by establishing freedom of enterprise in business; by abolishing primogeniture; and by freeing Protestants and Jews from religious and civil disabilities.

Largely as a result of these revolutionary changes France was involved in civil and foreign wars. As a consequence, the liberal state of 1791 foundered. What followed was the Reign of Terror, the Directory, and finally the dictatorship of Napoleon. Liberalism all but vanished.

The Restoration. With the restoration of the Bourbons in 1815, a new system of government was established by the *Charte,* a constitution granted by Louis XVIII. It organized France as a constitutional monarchy, with a parliament elected by a propertied suffrage. It provided for civil rights, equality before the law, religious toleration, and for the acceptance of most of the social changes made by the French Revolution. In a sense, the liberal state of 1791 was restored.

Nature of the Liberal State. In 1815, the historical beginning of the nineteenth century, the liberal state was established in Britain, France, and the United States. Though the systems of government varied in these countries they all adhered to the essentials of political liberalism. These were: (1) the making of laws by a representative legislature elected by qualified voters,

(2) the protection of civil liberty, or the natural rights of man, and (3) the right of peaceful opposition to the government, in and out of parliament. The liberal state was constitutional in that it provided for a system of distributing and limiting the powers of government with the object of preventing despotism, whether of one, of the few, or of the many. It reconciled freedom with authority through a Bill of Rights. Its basis, government by consent of the governed, created a moral community that bound all its members in a common aim to promote their common welfare. In these ways liberalism changed the very nature of the state from an organ of despotism to one of freedom.

Revolution was deemed justified to establish the liberal state. But it was to be a revolution to end all revolutions. Once established, the liberal state itself became the protector of the liberties of the citizens, and the chief mechanism of the peaceful progress of the nation. Hence, a revolution with the aim of overthrowing it has not been considered justifiable.

Liberals versus Reactionaries. The period, 1815-1870, witnessed a great upsurge of liberalism in the Western world. Its impact was predominantly political because the chief objective was to overthrow absolutism and to establish the liberal state. In Western Europe the liberal movement received the almost solid support of the middle class, now greater in wealth and in numbers because of the progress of the Industrial Revolution. The interests of this class demanded the abolition of the restrictions of feudalism and of mercantilism that hampered the development of commerce and industry. Revolutionary movements appeared with the object of creating a liberal state committed to the establishment of a free economy. The conflicts between the liberals and the reactionaries culminated in the great European upheaval, known as the Revolution of 1848.

Nationalism. There was another aspect to these struggles, namely nationalism. In modern times every people has either established itself as a sovereign, national state, or has passionately striven to do so. A "nation" may be better described than defined. It is a sovereign entity, independent of all other nations; its authority is limited by its frontiers. The political tie that binds a people into a nation is a common, equal citizenship; and the cultural tie, a common, national language. The supreme allegiance of every citizen is to his nation, whatever his class, race, or faith.

Liberal nationalism proclaimed the right of every people to "self-determination," of freedom from foreign rule. The nation, like the individual, was considered an autonomous entity, a "collective individual"; therefore, it had the right not only to be free but also independent. Inspired by the "principle of nationality," the people in divided Germany, as in divided Italy, sought to create a united fatherland. And the subject peoples in the Russian, Austrian, and Turkish Empires sought freedom from their oppressions in order to establish themselves as independent nations.

Classical Liberalism. As all other historical movements, liberalism likewise went through various stages of development. Its first stage, known as "classical" or "bourgeois" liberalism, can best be studied in France where it was established by the Revolution of 1830; and in Britain, by the Reform Bill of 1832. Classical liberalism developed policies, ideas, and attitudes which harmonized with the class interests of the bourgeoisie, and at the same time advanced greatly the cause of human freedom. In the new order all men were free and equal in the sense that all had equal civil rights. But all men did not have equal political rights. A property qualification for voting eliminated the working class from the suffrage, thereby making the bourgeoisie the ruling class. As a consequence the policies followed during the stage of classical liberalism were primarily directed to advance the interests of the bourgeoisie.

Classical Economy. Of these policies the most important concerned economic life. What has been called "economic liberalism" or "capitalism" derived its principles from the writings of the classical economists, a British school, the leading figures of which were David Ricardo (1772-1823) and Thomas Robert Malthus (1766-1834). They aimed to establish an economy in which the individual would have free scope to develop his energy and talents through freedom of enterprise and freedom of contract. Adam Smith was their original inspiration, but they developed his ideas into an integrated system that profoundly influenced economic thought during the nineteenth century.

The fundamental principle of the classical economists was derived from the idea that natural laws infallibly regulated economic transactions. Therefore, they upheld laissez faire, and even more dogmatically than had their master, Adam Smith. In a free market, prices of commodities would be determined by the natural, economic law of supply and demand. An unhampered, unregulated economy would increase production by encouraging enterprise. And it would lower prices through competition. Business would then prosper, and on the prosperity of business depended the prosperity of the nation. Capitalists would reap profits; laborers would find employment; farmers would receive good prices for their products; and landlords, high rents.

Labor, however, did not fare well in the scheme of economic liberalism. According to Ricardo, labor was a commodity, bought and sold like any other commodity in the free market. What the laborer received in wages, the "natural price," was a "subsistence wage," just enough to maintain him and his family. If he got more, it would be at the expense of profits. That would be bad for business, as from profits came the capital needed for increasing investments. Or it would be at the expense of another worker, as total wages could not exceed the sum known as the "wages fund," set aside by the employer for the payment of labor. As wages were determined chiefly by the cost of food, the classical economists favored the repeal of the Corn Laws, the tariff on food imports that kept the cost of food high in Britain. As a result, higher wages had to be paid. Cheap food from abroad would lower the cost of living; therefore, lower wages could be paid. The cost of production being lower, profits would be higher; hence, the amount left for investment would be greater. Cheap food, according to the classical economists, would lead to national prosperity. Under this scheme the laborer was doomed to exist on a mere subsistence level. (*See Reading No. 19.*)

Freedom of contract between individuals was considered essential to the functioning of the free economy. Buyer and seller, employer and employed, landlord and tenant were to be free to negotiate the terms of their contracts, and contracts thus negotiated would generally prove beneficial to both parties. Combinations, whether of labor or capital, were deemed conspiracies and, as such, violations of the freedom of contract. For this reason economic liberalism opposed trade unions as stoutly as it did industrial monopolies.

To the doctrines of classical economy Malthus contributed his famous "principle of population," known as "Malthusianism," which further doomed the laborer to his fate. According to this principle, there is a natural, universal tendency for the increase of population to outrun the increase of the food supply. The balance between population and food supply had been maintained by famines, wars, pestilences, and other calamities. Though these evils have lessened, argued Malthus, the "principle of population" continues to operate. Should the worker, whom Malthus considered ignorant and shiftless, receive an increase in wages he would raise a larger family. There would then be more workers competing for jobs. As a result, wages would fall, and the worker would be back again to a mere subsistence level. All efforts on the part of government, of charity, or of trade unions to ameliorate permanently the lot of the poor, according to Malthus, would be nullified by the "principle of population." (*See Reading No. 20.*)

To justify the economic as well as the political subordination of the workers in a free society, gradations in status and in well-being were ascribed by the bourgeois liberals to natural inequality among men. Riches were the reward for capacity, foresight, prudence, and enterprise; and poverty, the punishment for those who lacked these virtues. It followed logically that men of property were the only ones fit to rule the nation; therefore the justification of propertied suffrage. The bourgeoisie, having no privileges, as had the landed aristocracy, considered itself to be the "people" in the truest sense. All during the period of classical liberalism, initiative, leadership, and driving power in practically all areas of life came from the bourgeoisie.

Laissez Faire. The state, in view of the bourgeois liberals, occupied an important but negative position in relation to society. It was not to intervene in economic life except as the guardian of the free market. As such its functions were to enforce contracts, to punish frauds, and to maintain a stable currency. This laissez faire doctrine forbade intervention by the government on behalf of the capitalists as mischievous meddling; and on behalf of the workers as a futile effort to negate the consequences of the working of natural laws. This political philosophy was clearly and frankly formulated by Herbert Spencer, the famous British sociologist and scientist. (*See Reading No. 21.*) However, the state did have a role as reformer: to clear away the obstacles on the road to a free society by abolishing serfdom, slavery, class privileges, and monopolistic guilds and corporations. With these reforms would be liberated the natural forces in life making for freedom and prosperity.

As in so many other instances in history the actual practice did not carry out the theory. Laissez faire was not fully applied in any Western nation during the period of classical liberalism. For one reason or another the state did sometimes intervene in economic matters by granting subsidies to railways, by laying protective tariffs, and by enacting factory reforms.

Elasticity of Liberalism. As a political system liberalism has been distinctive in its capacity for self-transformation. Whether monarchical or republican in form the liberal state developed a power hitherto unknown, that of political elasticity in order to accommodate itself to changing conditions and opinions. It has advocated different policies at different times. Unlike the absolute state, whether that of divine right monarchy, or of military dictatorship, or of totalitarianism, the liberal state made provision for peaceful change through periodic elections. It, therefore, made impossible permanent rule by any special interest, by any favored class, or by any self-chosen elite.

Classical liberalism, because of its bourgeois class interest, could not be expected to promote the democratic forces that were emerging. Popular sovereignty, implied in the creation of the liberal state, became the generating principle of a popular movement in favor of manhood suffrage. It realized an early success in America where the northern and western states granted the vote to all men during the Jacksonian period of the 1830's. In Western Europe the workers threatened revolution unless their demand for the suffrage was granted. This demand received the support of the progressively-minded bourgeois liberals; and, in Britain, also of many conservatives. In this new climate of opinion the emergence of democracy could not long be delayed. By the end of the nineteenth century, manhood suffrage was virtually established by most of the nations of Western Europe. Equality before the ballot box was now added to equality before the law.

Democratic Liberalism. Liberalism now entered a new stage, democratic liberalism, or democracy. Hitherto antithetical in their meaning, the terms "liberalism" and "democracy" became interchangeable. New reforms were inaugurated that aimed to bring greater equality in social and economic life. Free, public, elementary schools were established, and illiteracy in Western Europe was on the way to extinction. Labor unions were emancipated from restrictive legislation. Even more important was the inauguration of systems of social security.

Fall of Laissez Faire. Democratic liberalism repudiated laissez faire both in theory and in practice. It embarked on a policy of state intervention in matters economic for the benefit of the industrial workers. The latter had benefited from the great progress of industry, but only to a limited degree. Large numbers of them still lived in a state of extreme poverty, even in prosperous England, France, and Germany. Worse than poverty was insecurity because unemployment, sickness, disability, and old age deprived many of their livelihood. They had the vote and civil liberty, but were miserable and helpless. Widespread discontent found expression in the rapid growth of socialism. The masses were not content to be "sovereign and miserable."

The pioneer of social reform was the semi-liberal German Empire, and for reasons which will be explained in a future chapter. During 1906-1914 Britain and France followed Germany's example, but for different reasons. These nations, inspired by the ideals of democratic liberalism, recognized the responsibility of the state for the economic welfare of the workers. (*See Reading No. 22.*)

Social Liberalism. The new liberalism continued to advance on the road of social reform. During the period from the end of the First World War to the mid-twentieth century what has become known as the "Welfare State" was established in almost every Western nation. In this latest stage of liberalism the principle of equality was extended to matters economic. By economic equality was meant, not equal division of wealth, but the abolition of poverty, at least the worst aspects of it, and a more equitable distribution of the national income through higher wages and through larger social benefits financed by heavy taxation on high incomes of individuals and corporations. A frontal attack on poverty was launched which, according to the social liberalism of the Welfare State, was a problem to be solved through the ordered liberties of democracy. The classical economists had emphasized economic insecurity as the fundamental motive for the production of wealth, maintaining that without fear of want men would not work or save. But the leading economists of the Welfare State—notably the Britons, John M. Keynes and William Beveridge—emphasized economic security, to be achieved by legislation favorable to full employment at high wages and by social reform, as the incentive to increased production. Laissez faire, a revolutionary doctrine in the eighteenth century, a liberal one in the nineteenth, was repudiated as a reactionary one in the twentieth.

The Welfare State aimed to realize greater security and well being for all. Social reform had hitherto been remedial in character, designed to tide over emergencies. Under the Welfare State it became an integral part of national life. The scope of social security was extended and the benefits enlarged with the object of protecting the working population against the hazards of economic life. Regulation of wages and hours of labor placed a minimum on the former and a maximum on the latter. Nationalization of public utilities had, to a limited extent, existed before 1914. Now it was widely extended especially in Britain, France, and Italy. Accumulation of large fortunes was severely curtailed by high income and inheritance taxes, especially in Britain and in the United States. Labor unions achieved a position of great power and influence. Hitherto, they had been tolerated, but now they were accepted as authoritative representatives of the workers. The social scale was tipped in favor of the workers by the new egalitarian society created by the Welfare State.

New Rights of Man. The old liberalism had concerned itself mainly with the protection of the individual against arbitrary acts of the government. The new liberalism sought to protect him against arbitrary acts of private organizations as well. In the highly mechanized, technological society of the twentieth century, non-political organs of power appeared in the forms of giant corporations and exclusive associations of all sorts. These could and did oppress the individual through controlling his livelihood. The task of the new liberalism was to protect the individual against oppression by private organizations. New rights were proclaimed by the Welfare State: the right to work, to a living wage, to rest and leisure, to all levels of education, and to equal opportunities for advancement, regardless of race, religion, or national origin. These new Rights of Man were incorporated in the post-war constitutions of the Fourth French Republic, the Italian Republic, and the German Federal Republic.

Universal Declaration of Human Rights. The newest liberalism found international expression in a resounding proclamation of both the old and new Rights of Man, issued by the United Nations. In 1948 the General Assembly adopted the Universal Declaration of Human Rights as "a common standard of achievement for all peoples and all nations." Some of the notable articles of the Declaration asserted that everyone had a right to social security, to equal pay for equal work, to a livelihood worthy of human dignity, to join a labor union, and to higher education on the basis of merit. (*See Reading No. 23.*) An ideal of social liberalism was now proclaimed for all mankind by a world body.

Progress of Liberalism. As liberalism passed from one stage to another its principles became more widespread, and at the same time more deeply rooted. The vote was extended from men of property to all men; and from all men to all women. Religious freedom was extended from the orthodox to the heretic; and from the heretic to the non-believer. Opportunity for self-advancement was extended from those of a favored ethnic group to those of other ethnic groups. In its various stages liberalism has pursued different policies, and has been espoused by different interests. Always, however, has it held fast to its fundamental principles of government by consent of the governed and of individual freedom under the law. Unless it adheres to these principles no system, whatever its form and whatever its aim, can rightly be called liberal.

— 4 —

LIBERALISM IN BRITAIN: FROM LAISSEZ FAIRE TO THE WELFARE STATE

England, a Liberal Nation. England is the birthplace of liberalism. There it was born; there its growth has been continuous; and there it has been accepted by virtually the entire nation. During the nineteenth and twentieth centuries English conservatives have not been reactionaries; once a reform was enacted they accepted it as part of the national system. And English radicals have not been revolutionists; they sought to accomplish their objectives by constitutional methods. Every substantial liberal gain that England made England kept.

English liberalism has had a distinctive national quality. It may be described as a complex of rights, privileges, and immunities won by the nation in its long history. From the time of Magna Charta the privileges of a minority were gradually extended until they became the rights of all Englishmen. Freedom, broadening down "from precedent to precedent" became the national tradition.

Restrictions on Liberalism. From the Revolution of 1688 to the Reform Bill of 1832 English liberalism presents a bare outline. Parliament, in theory representing the people, was chosen by few voters, chiefly property owners. The Bill of Rights dealt mainly with the rights of Parliament, and little with those of the individual citizen. The Toleration Act did not extend toleration to Catholics, Jews, and Unitarians. The press, in theory free, was limited by special taxes and by severe libel laws. Many important reforms had to be made before Britain would become a truly liberal nation.

Extension of Liberalism. Only Parliament could

make such reforms. But Parliament, prior to 1832, was controlled by a conservative aristocracy, through the restricted suffrage and the rotten borough system of representation. The movement to reform Parliament received powerful support from the rising middle class and from the numerous industrial workers. So great was the clamor for reform that important liberal measures were passed by the Tories, in control of Parliament. These were the repeal, in 1824, of the Combination Acts that prohibited trade unions; the repeal, in 1828, of the Test and Corporations Acts that imposed disabilities on the Nonconformists; and, most important of all, Catholic emancipation, in 1829, which repealed the religious, civil, and political disabilities of Catholics.

New Pattern of Liberalism. These early reforms served to stimulate a demand for greater and more extensive ones. As a result of the great industrial changes in Britain during the first half of the nineteenth century the new climate of opinion was instrumental in generating a body of doctrines that became the pattern of nineteenth century liberalism. It comprehended a philosophy of life known as Utilitarianism, proclaimed by Jeremy Bentham (1748-1832); a program of political reform, known as Philosophic Radicalism drawn up by James Mill (1773-1836); and a program of economic reform, the work of John Bright (1811-1889) and Richard Cobden (1804-1865), leaders of what became known as the Manchester School.

Utilitarianism. According to Utilitarianism the primary forces controlling human action were the desire for pleasure and the avoidance of pain. These natural forces, argued Bentham, governed men in all they did, said, and thought. All his life man strives to achieve happiness which, according to Bentham, is the outcome of material well-being, and each individual is the best judge of what is conducive to his happiness. (*See Reading No. 24.*)

Utilitarianism laid the foundation for a new morality, based on the "Greatest Happiness" principle. It held that those actions were right that tended to promote the greatest happiness of the greatest number, and were wrong if they did not tend to do so. Bentham and his followers were convinced that the then-existing institutions and laws of Britain tended to promote the happiness of the few and the misery of the many. Hence, they advocated the abolition of antiquated institutions and outworn laws and the repudiation of confining traditions and customs that hampered man in the pursuit of his happiness. The new society envisioned by the Utilitarians would be one in which the individual would have full and free opportunity to advance his own interests, to express his own opinions, and to go his own way.

Philosophic Radicalism. Closely related to the Utilitarians were the Philosophic Radicals, a group of "eggheads" in politics. Though few in number and not a political party, they exerted a profound influence on public opinion. They advocated radical, *i.e.* root reforms in the political and social order as the only alternative to revolution. Such reforms could be made peacefully, they contended, provided the control of Parliament passed from the hands of the aristocrats to those of the middle class. James Mill, the leading spokesman of the Philosophic Radicals, bitterly attacked aristocratic influences in church, state, and empire, the "sinister interests," who ruled Britain. He formulated a comprehensive radical program, including expansion of the suffrage, abolition of rotten boroughs, limitation of the power of the House of Lords, secret ballot, separation of church and state, and self-government for the colonies. At the same time he was a staunch upholder of property rights and of a propertied suffrage. To Mill the middle class constituted the "public" and its interests, the public welfare.

Manchester School. In matters economic the Manchester School became the protagonist of the ideas of the classical economists. It was so called because the leaders of the School were identified with Manchester, the industrial capital of Britain. The statesman, Bright, and the propagandist, Cobden, translated their economic ideas into political policies that comprehended free trade, peace, and colonial self-government. Of paramount importance to them was free trade. They were convinced that once that was established in the world, it would be followed by universal peace and prosperity. The Manchester School opposed imperialism and favored loosening, if not actually cutting, ties that bound Britain to the Empire. In its view, imperialism led to war, to trade monopolies, and to political subjection. In matters domestic, the School upheld the doctrine of laissez faire and strongly opposed the intervention of the state on behalf of the workers, especially in the field of social legislation. To the efforts of the Manchester School may be credited the legislation repealing the Corn Laws and the extension of self-government to the colonies. (*See Reading No. 25.*)

Reform Bill of 1832. First and foremost, the advance of liberalism was bound up with the reform of Parliament. As the reform movement progressed it enlisted the powerful support of the Whig party, the custodian of the liberal tradition of the Revolution of 1688. So great was the demand for parliamentary reform that at times the nation was brought to the brink of revolution by popular upheavals. Parliament was finally induced to pass the historic Reform Bill of 1832.

This measure broadened the base of the liberal state, created in England by the Revolution of 1688. The suffrage was expanded to include the middle class; representation was made more equitable by a redistribution of seats; and the Lords became subordinate to the Commons. Though it was put through by the Whigs the Reform Bill of 1832 was loyally accepted by the Tories, thereby giving a distinctive stamp to British liberalism as being a national, not a party, tradition.

In the period that followed, the parties changed their names as well as their policies. The Liberals, formerly the Whigs, and the Conservatives, formerly the Tories, competed with each other for the control of the government by offering programs of reform. But neither opposed the constitutional system under which both functioned.

Era of Reform. During the period from 1832 to the 1870's, a series of reforms made Britain the very model of nineteenth-century liberalism. Some of these reforms were the work of the Liberal party; others, of the Conservative party. The Poor Law of 1833 reformed the system of public relief to the indigent. In 1833 Negro slavery was abolished in the colonies. The Corporations

Act of 1835 established local government on an elective basis. The Factory Laws of 1842 and 1847 regulated conditions of labor in mines and factories. The great economic reform of the period was the establishment of free trade by the repeal, in 1846, of the Corn Laws. In the field of religious reform, the emancipation of the Jews—as previously of the Catholics—was effected in 1858 by a law which permitted a Jew to become a member of Parliament. In the field of colonial reform British liberalism took a great step of progress. A far-reaching measure, the British North America Act (1867), supported by both parties, created a new pattern of self-government in the British Empire. It established Canada as a "Dominion" with almost complete self-government in domestic matters.

Gladstone. The great liberal statesman of the period was William E. Gladstone (1809-1898). As the leader of the Liberal party, Gladstone became the eloquent, upright, able champion of its policies. All his long public life he was an ardent reformer, yet cautious and prudent in his methods. When in office as Prime Minister, his chief concern was to promote "peace, retrenchment, and reform." Hardly a reform of importance was enacted in Britain during his public life for which he was not directly or indirectly responsible. Gladstone was English liberalism incarnate. Yet, because of his belief in laissez faire, he did little to advance social reform. His liberalism was to a great degree limited to political, educational, and religious reform. Gladstone was a deeply religious man, a devout member of the Church of England. It is important to note that English liberalism in all its stages was influenced by the Christian faith, in striking contrast to French liberalism which was non-religious, even anti-religious.

Mill. The philosopher of English liberalism who best expressed its ideas, political, social, and cultural, during this period was John Stuart Mill (1806-1873). He began as a bourgeois liberal but his vision constantly broadened until it encompassed universal suffrage, including women, social reform, and even the Welfare State. Mill combined open-mindedness, intellectual integrity, and a power of luminous exposition rarely found in one person.

As a democratic liberal, Mill renounced propertied suffrage. When any element of the population was excluded from the suffrage, he reasoned, its interests were always in danger of being disregarded. If considered at all, these interests were seen "with very different eyes from those of the persons" directly concerned. (*See Reading No. 26.*)

Mill came to the conclusion that political democracy, when established, would seek to promote the "greatest happiness of the greatest number" by advancing equality in the economic field. The distribution of wealth, in his view, did not depend on natural economic laws. He, therefore, repudiated laissez faire, and advocated state intervention as legitimate and necessary in order to bring about a more equitable distribution of wealth.

Mill was the unrivaled champion of individual liberty. His book, *On Liberty,* has been regarded as the best expression of the faith of a liberal in the progress of mankind through freedom of thought and action. The liberty of the individual was, according to Mill, the indispensable condition of his development. With it every reform could be achieved in time and peacefully; without it a reform was both tainted and uncertain. Individual liberty comprised liberty of thought and feeling, absolute freedom of opinion and sentiment on all subjects, and liberty to unite for any purpose not involving harm to others. (*See Reading No. 27.*)

Mill pleaded not only for freedom from state tyranny, but also for freedom from the constraints of social taboos and conventional ideas. He stressed the antithesis between society and the individual by asserting that the former tended to impose its own ideas and practices on those who who did not accept them, a tendency Mill considered to be as evil as repressive laws. Even false opinions, he maintained, should be tolerated by society as well as by the state because truth would gain vigor and significance as a result of being challenged and vindicated. He was convinced that, on the whole, the average man could be trusted to go his own way, to think his own thoughts, and to follow his own lights. In many ways Mill anticipated the democratic, and even the social, stage of liberalism.

Expansion of the Suffrage. Opposition to classical liberalism arose chiefly from the unenfranchised workers. It concentrated on the demand for manhood suffrage as the first essential to the attainment of democracy. This demand was one of the Six Points of the People's Charter, presented in 1848 as a petition to Parliament. (*See Reading No. 28.*) Though rejected, the demands of Chartism deeply influenced both political parties in favor of extending the franchise. The Reform Bill of 1867, giving the vote to the industrial workers, was put through by the Conservatives led by Benjamin Disraeli. Not to be outdone, the Liberals led by Gladstone put through the Reform Bill of 1884 giving the vote to the agricultural workers. Parliament was now elected by what was virtually manhood suffrage.

Democratic Liberalism. With the extension of the franchise, British liberalism entered the democratic stage. As after 1832 a number of liberal reforms followed, but this time in the interest of the workers. In 1870, an education law established a national system of free elementary public schools. The laws of 1871 and 1875 emancipated the trade unions from many legal restrictions. Later, in 1906, the trade unions were actually granted a privileged position in law; no damage suits could be brought against them arising from labor disputes. Religious reform advanced with the removal, in 1888, of the ban against the admission of atheists to Parliament; and in 1912, with the disestablishment of the Anglican church in Wales. Political reform advanced with the establishment, in 1872, of the secret ballot; and with the reduction of the House of Lords to political impotence by the Parliament Act of 1911. These reforms marked the advance of the newer, the democratic liberalism.

New Views of the State. Democracy inspired a new attitude toward the state. Unlike classical liberalism, which regarded the state as a necessary evil, democratic liberalism regarded it as a necessary good. Therefore, the power of the state was to be used to promote reforms in the economic order by removing the fear of undeserved misfortune, the lot of many because of unemployment, sickness, low wages, and old age. That spelled the doom of laissez faire. (*See Reading No. 29.*)

Democratic liberalism manifested itself vigorously in Britain during the first decade of the twentieth century. On the one hand, the Liberal party underwent a great transformation when it renounced laissez faire, and advocated social legislation. On the other hand, a new political party appeared, the British Labor party, committed to an even more radical program of social reform and to socialism as its ultimate goal. Both parties repudiated the antithesis, stressed by classical liberalism, between the individual and the state and between the individual and society. They sought to create a new order in which both state and society, by giving the individual more security, would also give him more freedom.

Social Reform. The Liberal party, backed by the Laborites, was in power from 1906 to 1916. Under the leadership of Herbert H. Asquith and David Lloyd George, democratic liberalism took the path of social reform. Notable among the social reforms were the Workmen's Compensation Act (1906), providing for compensation to workers for injury or disease sustained in the course of employment, the Old Age Pension Act (1908), giving government pensions to old workers; the Minimum Wage Act (1909), fixing minimum wages in certain industries; and the National Insurance Act (1911), providing benefits to workers during periods of sickness and unemployment. These measures and others vested the state with supervisory power over industry, with the aim of bringing about increased well-being and greater security for the workers.

Other Democratic Reforms. After the First World War, additional legislation increased the pace of the forward march of democratic liberalism in Britain. The suffrage was widely extended by the Reform Bill of 1918 (amended in 1928), establishing universal, equal suffrage for men and women. A great step was taken to liberalize the Empire when, in 1931, the Statute of Westminster made Britain and its Dominions "equal in status, in no way subordinate one to another" in any aspect of their domestic and foreign affairs.

The Labor Party. Party government underwent a highly important change when the Labor party came into power in 1923, succeeding the Liberal party as one of the two ruling parties, the other being the Conservative. The Laborites, headed by J. Ramsay MacDonald, were truly liberal in their political philosophy. Though committed to the establishment of socialism, they subscribed fully and uncompromisingly to the tenets of parliamentary government and civil liberty. As champions of democratic liberalism they were irreconcilably opposed to dictatorship, either by an individual, or by a group, or by a class. (*See Reading No. 30.*) Being socialists, the Laborites proposed to socialize industry gradually, and to pay a fair price to the owners of a private enterprise transferred to public ownership. With their faith in the "inevitability of gradualness" the Laborites aimed to reach their socialist goal by "parliamentary means and in progressive stages," thus preserving the liberal tradition.

Social Liberalism. The latest stage of liberalism, the Welfare State, was definitely established in Britain after the Second World War. As a result of the elections of 1945, the Labor party came into power and remained in power until 1951. The Labor ministry, headed by Prime Minister Clement Attlee, put through social legislation far more radical than that of the past. It aimed to guarantee a minimum level of subsistence for all, "from the cradle to the grave." The guiding principle was to distribute the national income in a manner that would allot "fair shares" to all elements of the population. (*See Reading No. 31.*) In line with this program, the following laws were enacted. The National Insurance Act (1946) provided allowances to insured workers during periods of sickness, disability, maternity, and unemployment; old age pensions and death benefits; and benefits to widows and orphans. The Industrial Injuries Act (1946) extended workmen's compensation for injury, disablement, and death sustained in the course of employment as a result of accident or industrial disease. The National Health Service Act (1946) provided for virtually free medicines and medical services to all, "from duke to dustman." Great advances were made in public ownership by the nationalization of the Bank of England, coal mines, railways, and over-seas air lines. Heavy income and inheritance taxes were laid on the wealthy. Secondary, and even higher, education was made accessible to the masses. A far-reaching housing program, aided by the government, provided homes for the workers at moderate cost. As a consequence of the establishment of the Welfare State, the traditional social order in Britain, with its sharp class divisions, was greatly modified. The extremes of wealth and poverty became less obvious with the significant rise in the standard of living of the worker. When, in 1951, the Conservative party came into power it maintained with little modification the Welfare State established by the Labor party.

Colonies Win Independence. As usual in Britain when a liberal advance was made at home, a like advance was made in the Empire. Southern Ireland, renamed "Eire," and Burma were granted complete independence. India, Pakistan, and Ceylon were granted Dominion status. Ghana (formerly the Gold Coast in Africa) became the first Negro colony to attain virtual independence as a Dominion. The admission of non-Europeans on the basis of equality with whites marked a notable liberalization of the Commonwealth.

Liberalism, a Bond of Union. British liberalism in all its stages has followed a pattern characteristic of the nation. It comprehended a critical attitude toward authority, both secular and religious; a belief in the worth and dignity of every person; a constant effort to improve living conditions gradually and peacefully; and a generous view of the capacity of the lower classes to rise to higher standards, both moral and intellectual. Liberalism spilled over at first into the Conservative party, which accepted reforms once made as part of the national heritage. Later, it spilled over into the Labor party, which became the legitimate successor of the Liberal party by accepting its method of progress through reform. In these ways liberalism became a national heritage, constituting the most powerful bond of union of the British people.

— 5 —

LIBERALISM IN FRANCE: PROGRESS AND REACTION

Character of French Liberalism. French liberalism was formulated in a different manner and proclaimed in a different spirit from that of British liberalism. Unlike the latter it had no deep historic roots, no tradition of freedom that "slowly broadens down from precedent to precedent." Its ideas, inspired by the philosophes of the eighteenth century, were formulated as principles to be applied in changing the existing order. These principles, proclaimed by the French Revolution, were universal in spirit, abstract in character, and revolutionary in application. The "principles of 1789" became the heritage not only of France but of the Continent generally.

Left and Right. Deep was the division in France between Left and Right, those who accepted and those who rejected the French Revolution. All during the nineteenth century the "two Frances" were locked in bitter conflict. Because of this "great divide" it was the fate of French liberalism to fight on two fronts: against reactionaries on the Right and against revolutionists on the Left. Hence, it was always on the alert, militant, even truculent. As a consequence, the progress of liberalism in France has been uncertain and checkered. Sometimes it made extraordinary advances; other times it suffered convulsive reactions.

The Restoration. This division manifested itself clearly and definitely during the Restoration (1815-1830). It took the form of a conflict between the Bourbon dynasty that sought to restore the absolutism of the Old Regime and the bourgeois liberals who sought to maintain intact the liberties granted by the *Charte.* In this conflict the French version of bourgeois liberalism was developed by the philosopher-statesmen, Pierre Paul Royer-Collard (1763-1845) and Benjamin Constant (1767-1830).

Bourgeois Liberalism. Royer-Collard became the eloquent spokesman of a political group, the Doctrinaires, that opposed the reactionary policies of the Bourbons. In his views of the power of parliament and of the nature of the franchise, Royer-Collard showed himself to be a moderate, even a cautious, bourgeois liberal. He repudiated the principle of popular sovereignty as expressed in the supremacy of parliament. Instead he proclaimed the principle of the "sovereignty of reason," working through the collaboration of king, peers, and parliament. The franchise he regarded not as a natural right but as a "function," entrusted to those qualified by property and education. What Royer-Collard upheld, without compromise whatever, was individual liberty, protected by an independent judiciary, buttressed by a free press, and guaranteed by the *Charte.* Whenever the Bourbon king "jumped out of the *Charte*" by suppressing civil liberty he encountered the valiant opposition of Royer-Collard.

Like Royer-Collard, Constant upheld liberal principles with staunch devotion. However, in developing these principles he gave them a broader base and a wider outlook. Constant knew well the mechanism of parliamentary government as it operated in Britain. In effect, he advocated a similar system of government based on the supremacy of parliament and ministerial responsibility. To the king he assigned the role of arbitrator in case of conflict between the various branches of the government. To make this system work, as in Britain, Constant realized the need for a limited number of political parties, well organized and strictly disciplined. Especially did he emphasize the role of an opposition party in his liberal scheme of government.

Revolution of 1830. During the reign of Charles X (1824-1830), the conflict between liberalism and reaction became irrepressible. It came to a head in 1830, when Charles suppressed the liberty of the press and dissolved a newly elected parliament. These moves roused widespread discontent, and the outcome was the July Revolution of 1830. The Bourbon Charles was overthrown, and the Orleanist Louis Philippe was made King. The new ruler assured his supporters of his earnest desire to reign as a constitutional monarch. Liberalism, to all appearances, triumphed over reaction.

The reign of Louis Philippe proved to be more liberal than the one that it had displaced. Parliament was made supreme in the government; ministerial responsibility was definitely recognized; and the suffrage was somewhat expanded by a reduction of the property qualification for voting.

More definitely now was bourgeois liberalism established in France. But it was more bourgeois than liberal. Political control was concentrated in the hands of the bourgeoisie, as a result of the elimination of aristocratic influences in the government and of the disfranchisement of the workers. The government under Louis Philippe thus became the efficient promoter of bourgeois interests almost to the exclusion of the interests of the other classes. Those in power were convinced that the new regime had at last ended both reaction and revolution in France by establishing a government that guaranteed both stability and freedom. Liberty, they contended, was now safe in the hands of those who had the capacity to maintain it, the bourgeoisie. (*See Reading No. 32.*)

Guizot. Bourgeois liberalism had as its chief spokesman the historian-statesman, François Guizot (1787-1874). He became Premier in 1840, and dominated the government until its downfall in 1848. Guizot was deeply and sincerely convinced that the bourgeoisie constituted the living forces of the nation. They alone had the capacity and the intelligence to rule; hence, liberty could be maintained only when the government was dominated by this class. But how could such a government in France be reconciled with the "principles of 1789"? In the view of Guizot the bourgeoisie was not a class, but the "people," at its truest and best. Under the free enterprise system, he argued, anyone could acquire property by engaging in business; and success was the prime test of capacity in the new economic order. (*See Reading No. 33.*) "Get rich," and you will enter the ranks of the rulers of the nation. Guizot doggedly opposed manhood suffrage on the ground that it would give political power to the economically unfit who would use the ballot to confiscate the property of the fit. Civil equality, or the equal protection of the laws, not political equality, or manhood suffrage was, according to Guizot, the natural right of all men. The regime of Louis Philippe, he asserted, took a middle ground between the extremes of reaction and revolution. It maintained the gains of the French Revolution and, at the same time, combatted the socialists who hoped to accomplish their aims by a new revolution.

All during the reign of Louis Philippe the bourgeois liberals devoted their energies to fighting their enemies, Left and Right. As a consequence, the reforms of the period were few and meagre. Liberalism acquired a bad name in France; it was branded as the philosophy of a selfish, capitalist oligarchy. Parliament was distrusted as a bourgeois institution, especially by the socialists who avowed their purpose to destroy, not to reform, it. The regime also roused the hostility of the democratic liberals, who hoped for greater progress under a parliament, elected by manhod suffrage.

Tocqueville. The great spokesman of the democratic liberals was the political philosopher, Alexis de Tocqueville (1805-1859). His book, *Democracy in America,* was a notable contribution to political philosophy as well as a penetrating analysis of American democracy of the Jacksonian period.

Tocqueville detested the rule of a capitalist oligarchy under bourgeois liberalism as strongly as he detested the authoritarian rule of an absolute monarch. A "liberal of a new order" he was convinced that democracy was inevitable because of the passion of men for equality, "ardent, insatiable, incessant, invincible." According to Tocqueville, manhood suffrage was the only legitimate source of political power. With remarkable foresight he realized that manhood suffrage, once granted, would bring a demand for the abolition of poverty. The development of the principle of equality, he regarded as a "providential fact," in that it was universal, lasting, and inevitable. Therefore, the legislator should devote his energies primarily to the improvement of the lot of the workers through social reform. The solution of the great problem that now confronted mankind hinged, according to Tocqueville, on the reconciliation of popular rule with respect for property, for individual freedom, and for religion. He was convinced that America had solved this problem, but was uncertain whether France would succeed in solving it because of the conflict between the revolutionists and the reactionaries. (*See Reading No. 34.*)

Revolution of 1848. Opposition to the Bourgeois Monarchy became ever stronger and ever more widespread. It was concentrated on the demand for manhood suffrage. Convinced that democratic liberalism would be the gateway to socialism, Guizot was obdurate in his refusal to make any concession to this demand. Instead, he resorted to despotic measures and to political corruption to suppress opposition. Revolution appeared the only way to get rid of the hated regime.

The situation reached a climax with the February Revolution of 1848. Under the leadership of democratic liberals, an uprising overthrew Louis Philippe and the regime for which he stood. In its place was established the Second Republic, based on manhood suffrage.

Revival of Bonapartism. A situation soon arose that spelled the doom of democratic liberalism. The Republicans, now in power, were confronted by two deadly enemies: the Bonapartists on the Right, who wished to restore the glories of the First Empire; and the Socialists on the Left, who wished to inaugurate the "cooperative commonwealth." An uprising of the Paris workers took place, the "June Days," foreboding a new Reign of Terror. It was suppressed, but the Republic was doomed. Out of fear of a socialist revolution France turned to a "savior," Louis Napoleon Bonaparte, who first overthrew the Second Republic by the coup d'état of 1851, and then made himself Emperor in 1852. Under the Second Empire, liberalism was subdued and remained quiescent for twenty years.

The Third Republic. In France a national crisis not infrequently led to a change in the system of government. With the defeat of France in the Franco-Prussian War (1870-1871) the Second Empire went out of existence. During the period 1871-1875, a great struggle raged in the National Assembly, elected to form a new government. On the Right were the Royalists determined to restore the Bourbon monarchy; and on the Left were the Republicans equally determined to establish a democratic republic. What made the situation even more critical was the Paris Commune (1871), an uprising of the Socialist workers far greater than that of the "June Days" of 1848. It was mercilessly suppressed by the National Assembly, thereby ending the danger of revolution. But the danger of reaction remained. Liberalism triumphed when the moderate and radical Republicans united against the Royalists. In 1875, the National Assembly adopted a constitution which established France as a Republic, based on manhood suffrage.

Democratic Liberalism. With the creation of the Third Republic, liberalism in France experienced a new birth. It became known as radicalism, the creed of Léon Gambetta (1838-1882), acclaimed as the father of the Third French Republic. Gambetta's program demanded the establishment of a republic ruled by an all powerful legislature elected by manhood suffrage, the "master of us all"; freedom of speech, of the press, and of assembly; free public, secular schools; separation of church and state; and maintenance of the rights of property. (*See Reading No. 35.*) To carry out this "radical" program Gambetta founded the Radical party (later known as the Radical Socialist party) that exercised a predominant influence in formulating the policies of the Third Republic.

All during its life of seventy years the Third Republic was engaged in desperate struggles for survival. Almost every decade witnessed a great crisis threatening its very existence, and the issue always centered around liberalism, democratic and republican, against reactionary royalism. The first of these struggles was the MacMahon affair of the 1870's. Marshal MacMahon, the Royalist President, sought to overthrow the Republic by dissolving the Chamber. Despite the coercion of the voters by the government, the elections of 1877 resulted in an overwhelming victory for the Republicans. MacMahon later resigned, and was succeeded by a Republican.

The next crisis took place in the 1880's with the threat of a coup d'état by the popular General Boulanger. But the danger to the Republic was averted when the General, charged with treason, fled the country and committed suicide.

By far the greatest crisis of the Third Republic took place during the famous Dreyfus Affair (1894-1906). Over the guilt or innocence of Captain Alfred Dreyfus, a great struggle raged, the outcome of which involved the very existence of the Republic. All the forces of reaction, royalism, militarism, and clericalism combined to uphold the verdict pronounced against Dreyfus by a military court, which found him guilty of treason. All the forces of liberalism, from the most moderate to the most radical, combined to demand a revision of the verdict, in the belief that Dreyfus was innocent and had been condemned because of anti-Semitism. The innocence of Dreyfus became the rallying cry of the great battle for the Republic fought by his supporters.

The real issue was the survival of the liberal Third Republic. In 1899 an extraordinary Ministry was formed with the object of revising the verdict against Dreyfus. It was headed by Premier Waldeck-Rousseau, and contained representatives of every republican group in the Chamber. For the first time, a Socialist, Alexandre Millerand, became a minister. As in the former crises liberals of all schools concentrated on the defense of the Republic. This Ministry began the rehabilitation of Dreyfus, who finally was declared innocent of any act of treason by a civil tribunal. With the vindication of Dreyfus liberalism achieved a resounding victory. Royalism became so discredited that it ceased to have any importance. The Third Republic was now safe.

Clericalism versus Anti-Clericalism. The conflict between liberalism and reaction had a religious as well as a political aspect. During the Restoration the influence of the Catholic church, officially established by Napoleon's Concordat of 1801, was used by the Bourbons to bolster their rule. As the liberals opposed the monarchy so did they oppose clericalism, or the intervention of the church in politics and government. Generally the liberals were rationalists, or free thinkers, who favored the lay, or secular state, and the restriction of the church to purely religious matters. During the nineteenth century, royalism and clericalism became almost synonymous in France, as did liberalism and anti-clericalism.

During the three "Affairs" the Catholics strongly supported the royalists. They feared that the Third Republic, inspired by the principles of the French Revolution, would attack the church as had the First Republic. To the Catholics the Republic was the avowed enemy, and the monarchy, the traditional friend and protector. It was the hostility of the clericals to the Republic that inspired Gambetta's famous slogan, *Le cléricalisme, voilà l'ennemi!* ("Clericalism, that is the enemy!")

After the Third Republic was definitely established, a number of laws were passed aimed to make France a secular state. A law of 1884 declared that marriages to be valid had to be legalized by a magistrate. Another law permitted divorce. A national system of elementary education, free and secular, was established by the Ferry Laws (1881-1886). The new school system had political as well as educational objectives in that the pupils were taught loyalty to the Republic and to the liberal principles for which it stood. By far the most important anti-clerical law, passed in 1905 as a result of the Dreyfus Affair, was the law separating church and state. Clericalism thereafter ceased to have much importance in France.

Socialists Accept Liberalism. At last French liberalism found a secure abiding place. The Third Republic proved to be the most stable government in France since the French Revolution. It enjoyed a longer life than had the preceding two monarchies, two Republics, and two Empires. New forces in the life of the nation served to give added strength to liberalism. One was the support of the industrial workers. The suppression of the Commune convinced them that revolution was outmoded as a method of establishing socialism. They forsook the barricade, and organized socialist parties to win seats in parliament. What strengthened their confidence in the Republic was the adoption of the trade union law of 1884. This law completely emancipated the trade unions from regulations designed to hamper their activities. In 1896, the Socialists adopted a platform known as the Saint-Mandé Program, declaring that socialism should now devote itself to the gradual attainment of its objectives through parliamentary methods. (*See Reading No. 36.*) In other words, French socialism definitely abandoned the method of revolution and adopted the method of liberalism. This new attitude became evident during the Dreyfus Affair, when the Socialist party, under its leader, Jean Jaurès, became part of the Left bloc to defend the Republic. It played a highly important role in the revision of the Dreyfus Affair and in the enactment of the reforms that followed.

Social Liberalism. For long the Republic, fighting for its life against the royalists, had been tardy in the sphere of social reform. After the Dreyfus Affair, state intervention on behalf of the workers displaced laissez faire as the philosophy of French liberalism. Radical factory reforms and workmen's compensation laws were passed. Most important of these reforms was the Pension Law of 1910, giving pensions to retired workers.

These reforms served the Republic well. During the First World War the government received the support of practically every party. To preserve this national solidarity after the war additional social reforms were passed. In 1930 a comprehensive social insurance system was adopted, which provided benefits for sickness, invalidity, maternity, old age, and, in case of death of the insured, to his survivors. In 1932 a family allowance law compelled employers to pay bonuses to those of his workers with children. Even more advanced was the new liberalism of the Socialist ministry of Léon Blum (1936-1937). Laws were adopted establishing a 40-hour work week; paid vacations; and collective agreements on a nation-wide scale between unions and employers.

The Fourth Republic. The Third Republic went out of existence as a result of the defeat of France in the Second World War. In 1946 the Fourth French Republic was established by a popularly elected constitutional convention. The new constitution was drawn up on a pattern of advanced political and social liberalism. Supreme authority was vested in a lower house, the National Assembly, elected by universal suffrage; for the first time women were enfranchised. It had the sole power to legislate and to control the ministry; the upper house, the Council, was given only nominal power. Along with the traditional rights of man, the constitution proclaimed the right to work; the right of labor to organize and to strike; the right to economic security; the right to education on all levels; and the right to nationalize monopolistic industries. Laws were passed making the social security laws more liberal; and extending nationalization to include the Bank of France, coal mines, gas and electricity, and some of the automobile works. These reforms established the Welfare State in France.

As in Britain the triumph of liberalism meant the application of its principles to the colonies. The constitution of the Fourth Republic proclaimed "equality of rights and duties without distinction of race or religion." This principle was applied to the inhabitants of Algeria, where the Moslems were granted citizenship. Measures were adopted extending local self-government in the various colonies. In 1956 Morocco and Tunis were granted independence on terms similar to those of a Dominion in the British Commonwealth.

In the Fourth Republic, French liberalism again has to fight on two fronts: against the Communists on the Left and against semi-Fascist groups on the Right. But this time three elements, hitherto mutually antagonistic, have consolidated into a powerful liberal Center to defend the Republic. These are a Catholic group, the Popular Republicans, the Radical Socialists, and the Socialists. All of them have been loyal to the Republic, faithful to the democratic process, committed to the maintenance of the Welfare State, and favorable to the gradual abolition of colonialism. The Fourth Republic has now assumed the role of preserving and advancing the cause of liberalism in France.

— 6 —

LIBERALISM IN ITALY: MONARCHICAL AND REPUBLICAN

Background. In Italy liberalism had an early beginning but an uncertain existence. Its primal source was the Renaissance, secular, individualistic, skeptical, that profoundly influenced the making of the Italian liberal mind. During the nineteenth century, the supporters of liberalism in Italy, as elsewhere, came largely from the middle class. But that class in Italy was small; hence, it did not have the drive and power that the large middle class of Britain and France had. The mass of the nation consisted of impoverished, illiterate peasants, indifferent to politics; and of poorly paid, discontented workers inclined to seek salvation in social revolution. For these reasons liberalism failed to strike deep roots in the nation as a whole. Whenever a critical situation arose in Italy liberalism stood to suffer.

Liberal Nationalism. Unlike Britain and France, Italy had first to solve the problem of unifying the nation before establishing the liberal state. In 1815, Italy was a "geographical expression," divided into seven independent parts, each ruled despotically. What made the problem of unity even more difficult was that one part, Lombardy-Venetia, belonged to Austria; and another part, the States of the Church, was ruled by the pope. Any effort to incorporate these parts into a united Italy would rouse the hostility of a powerful nation, Austria, and of the influential head of the Catholic church.

These difficulties served, if anything, to bind more closely the national and liberal movements. Nationalism became the driving force of Italian liberalism of whatever school, bourgeois, democratic, or social. The makers of united Italy, Mazzini, Cavour, King Victor Emmanuel, and Garibaldi, were all liberals who ardently sought to unite their country in freedom. Liberal nationalism was Italy's contribution to the cause of human freedom.

Mazzini. The greatest exponent of liberal nationalism was Joseph Mazzini (1805-1872). His unique gifts of poetic imagination, literary skill, and zealous devotion served greatly to advance the cause to which he dedicated his life. Mazzini's activity in behalf of Italian unification was motivated by his philosophy of nationalism, which was universal in outlook. The nation, according to Mazzini, is intermediate between the individual and humanity; as such it gives significance to the individual and direction to civilization. On the achievement of nationhood by every people, large and small, depends the progress of mankind. Hence, divided peoples should be united, and subject peoples, freed. To Mazzini a nation was not primarily "a mere zone of territory" but "the idea to which it gives birth." Each and every nation is, therefore, a unique entity, having its special mission which constitutes its reason for existence. Only if united, asserted Mazzini, would Italy carry out its mission and make its special contribution to modern civilization. (*See Reading No. 37.*)

Though an ardent nationalist Mazzini was also an internationalist. He loved Italy "above all earthly things," and at the same time admired other nations, especially France and England. The cause of the subject peoples of his day, such as the Poles and the Hungarians, enlisted his enthusiastic support because they were striving for independence.

Mazzini's nationalism was inseparable from his liberalism. He was deeply convinced that nationalism would find its best and truest expression in a democratic republic, the only logical and legitimate form of government. The man who does not vote "ceases to be a citizen." This system, based on the principles of national sovereignty, "knows no castes or privileges save those of Genius and Virtue; no proletariat or aristocracy of land or finance but only abilities and active forces." It is important to note that Mazzini's liberalism derived from the democratic, not from the bourgeois, school. He was averse to the laissez faire policies and to the system of propertied suffrage of bourgeois liberalism. He may be considered the founder of Italian democracy in its advanced stage of radical social reform, as he advocated social security legislation for the benefit of the workers. Mazzini's vision of a united Italy was republican, democratic, and social.

As nationalism was to Mazzini the central fact of modern history he developed a philosophy of progress, that visualizes the future as a united world of liberal nations dedicated to peace. Progress, he asserted, results from the conflict between generations, not that between classes, faiths, races, or nations. The rising generation—ardent, idealistic, discontented—is always in conflict with the older generation—cautious, traditional, and practical. In other words, youth is liberal; old age, conservative. The better future comes only with the victory of the younger over the older generation. Mazzini actually conceived plans of organizing the youth in various lands to be the vanguard of progress. He founded Young Italy, consisting of educated young men who dedicated themselves to the unification of Italy as a democratic republic. He also founded Young Europe, an international society of youth dedicated to the liberation of subject peoples. Mazzini's idea became the inspiration of radical youth movements throughout the world. Its influence is felt even today.

Cavour. A liberal nationalist of quite another sort was Camillo Benso, Count di Cavour (1810-1861). Unlike Mazzini, Cavour was not a thinker but a statesman, not an idealist but a man of affairs. He devised policies inspired by the bourgeois liberalism of England. His economic views were derived from the Manchester school; and his political views, from the Whigs. Cavour was convinced that only by following a moderate course could Italy be united and stay united. This course meant the establishment of united Italy as a constitutional monarchy with a parliament controlled by the propertied classes. By providing a new unifying center, parliament would become the supreme institution for fusing the Italians into a common nation. "In the work of Cavour," writes

Guido de Ruggiero in his *The History of European Liberalism,* "we feel for the first time in Italian history the living spirit of the modern Liberal state; the State which feeds upon mighty conflicts, which reconciles violent passions any one of which in isolation would be destructive and disastrous, while each, in its union with the others, is an element of life and progress."

Revolution of 1848. Both the radicalism of Mazzini and the moderation of Cavour constituted integral parts of the liberal movement to unite Italy, known as the *Risorgimento* (Resurrection). It reached a high point in the Revolution of 1848. The turn of events in Piedmont-Sardinia was to prove highly significant for the future of Italy. There King Charles Albert voluntarily promulgated a liberal constitution, the famous *Statuto,* providing for a parliament elected by property owners; ministerial responsibility; and civil liberties. This constitution was loyally maintained by his son and successor, Victor Emmanuel. Piedmont-Sardinia emerged from the Revolution of 1848 the only liberal state in Italy.

Cavour Unites Italy. In 1852 Cavour became Prime Minister of Piedmont-Sardinia, determined to make his country the liberal protagonist of unification. In order to establish liberalism on a more solid basis he sought to increase the urban population by promoting industrialization. He put through anti-clerical legislation to make the state supreme over the church in civil matters. He steadfastly maintained the constitutional system, thereby firmly establishing Piedmont-Sardinia as a liberal state under a liberal monarch. Cavour's ultimate objective was to make Piedmont-Sardinia the basis of a united Italy, and Victor Emmanuel its future king.

Cavour proved to be a statesman of the first order. His extraordinary diplomacy won allies for Piedmont-Sardinia; together they succeeded in expelling Austria from Italy. His steadfast loyalty to constitutional government brought him the support of many republicans, notably that of Garibaldi. The result, finally achieved in 1870, was a united Italy with Victor Emmanuel as King, with Rome as the capital, and the *Statuto* as the constitution. United Italy was a signal triumph of liberal nationalism.

Bourgeois Liberalism. The history of liberalism in

united Italy has not been an heroic tale like that of the *Risorgimento*. During the period of 1870-1914, liberalism did not progress steadily from the bourgeois to the democratic stage as it did in England and in France. For long the electorate was narrowly restricted; manhood suffrage was not adopted until 1912. Illiteracy was widespread, and popular education advanced slowly. Vast numbers suffered extreme poverty, but social reforms were few and meagre. Parliament was the scene of squabbles between factions and politicians eager for office. Whether the parties of the Right or of the Left were in power they were chiefly concerned with political manipulation, not with the solution of national problems. During this period no public figure appeared worthy of being designated as a great statesman.

Unsolved Problems. Italy did have problems, and very grave ones, that involved the very existence of the liberal regime. Highly important was the Roman Question, involving relations between church and state. After Rome became the capital, the Law of Papal Guarantees was passed, giving special privileges to the pope in the Vatican, a district in Rome reserved for his activities. The pope refused to recognize this law; he wished to be restored to his former position as ruler of Rome. He set himself in opposition to the Italian government by claiming to be the "Prisoner of the Vatican." Italy, being almost entirely Catholic, the hostility of the pope constituted, for a time at least, a threat to national unity.

Another serious problem concerned the backwardness of the South. It was primarily an agricultural region, yet without the advantages of modern farming. The soil was poor. The land was divided into large estates, the *latifundia,* owned by absentee landlords. The peasants on these estates were generally underpaid, illiterate laborers, whose one hope lay in emigration.

Another problem existed in the industrialized North. The pace of development in this region was slowed down by the lack of a sufficient supply of natural resources, such as coal and iron. A fairly large working class existed, but as industrial productivity was relatively small, wages were low; hours of labor, long; and unemployment, frequent.

Italian liberalism did not come to grips with these problems. The Roman Question remained unsolved. Almost nothing was done to improve the agrarian economy of the South. Mild factory reforms were passed, and then rarely enforced. The Liberal parties became expert in the art of avoiding serious issues, contenting themselves with sonorous declarations of liberal principles. Liberalism in Italy became a byword for weakness and evasion.

Revolutionary Discontent. Mass poverty and heavy taxation resulted in widespread discontent. Strikes of agricultural laborers in the South and of industrial laborers in the North were so violent that they took on the character of revolutionary uprisings. Owing to the weakness of liberalism, revolutionary movements enlisted the support of many. A large Socialist party appeared in Parliament. The trade unions were won over to syndicalism. Anarchism of the most violent sort became the creed of secret societies that plotted the overthrow of the government. Fear of revolution pervaded the propertied elements of the nation. Whenever a crisis arose the government managed to survive, either by stern repression or by mild concessions. After each crisis, however, it became weaker, with the result that there was manifested a growing lack of confidence in its ability, even in its willingness, to make a resolute effort to solve the problems that confronted the nation. Italian liberalism during this period lived precariously amidst a fear-stricken bourgeoisie, an indifferent peasantry, and a hostile proletariat.

When, in 1915, Italy entered the First World War on the side of the Allies, patriotic sentiment united the nation in support of the government. But this unity was broken with the ending of the war. Patriotic sentiment was deeply affronted by the scant regard paid by the Allies to Italy's claim for a larger share of the conquered territory than she had received. Economic conditions, always bad in Italy, now became much worse because of inflation, bankruptcy, and unemployment resulting from the war. A revolutionary movement, inspired by communism, culminated in 1920 in a general strike of all labor, creating a national crisis. The workers seized factories, and ousted the owners. Though the strike was settled, property owners remained apprehensive. They feared that the government, which had been weak and faltering during the crisis, would not be determined and resolute in combatting any future revolutionary uprising. They began to seek ways and means outside the government to insure their security.

Fall of the Liberal State. Under these circumstances many saw salvation in a new movement, fascism, and beheld a savior in its leader, the ex-Socialist, Benito Mussolini (1883-1945). The Fascists bitterly denounced the liberal state as weak in defending national interests, and as irresolute in protecting property rights. Mussolini threatened to overthrow the government by a coup d'état unless it was turned over to him unconditionally. It was no historic accident that the storm of fascism destroyed liberalism in Italy where its roots lay so near the surface.

In 1922, King Victor Emmanuel III appointed Mussolini as Premier, though the Fascist party had no majority in Parliament. As a party the Fascists had received only about five per cent of the votes in the elections of 1921. Once in power Mussolini promptly set up a Fascist party dictatorship. The Italian liberal state, as established in 1870, was destroyed. Liberal ideas were stridently repudiated, and liberal practices were sternly suppressed. During the Fascist regime, from 1922 to 1943, Mussolini stood defiant "over the dead body of Liberty."

Restoration of the Liberal State. The Fascist regime was overthrown as a result of the defeat of Italy in the Second World War. Italian liberalism experienced a new birth with the establishment, in 1947, of a republic in place of the monarchy. Its constitution declared that "Italy is a democratic Republic founded on labor." A system of government was adopted, the chief features of which were: a president with nominal powers; a parliament of two houses, both elected by universal suffrage (including women); and a ministry responsible to parliament. An elaborate Bill of Rights guaranteed the traditional rights of man, and, in addition, the new social rights, such as the right to work, to social security and to organize trade unions. Equality before the law was decreed, without distinction of sex, race, faith or opinion. A supreme court was established with power to interpret the constitution. Another novel feature of the constitution was the right granted to the various regions to establish local parliaments. Italian liberalism was now definitely democratic and social.

Progress under the Republic. The elections of 1948 and of 1953 revealed that the majority of Italians supported the Republic. As elsewhere, however, a new enemy, communism, emerged to threaten the liberal state. In these elections the Communist party, together with its allies, received about one-third of the popular vote. Unlike the liberalism of the monarchy, that of the Republic resolutely determined to solve the grave problems confronting the nation. The Roman Question was finally settled by the constitution, which recognized the pope as the sovereign ruler of the newly created "State of the Vatican City." Notable progress has been achieved in solving the land problem in the South by promoting peasant proprietorship. Public education has been extended so that literacy has become practically universal. Most notable, however, has been the application of the principles of the Welfare State by the enactment of comprehensive social security laws, and by the public ownership of a large part of industry. An accelerated development of commerce and industry—aided by American gifts, loans, and investments—has been transforming Italy into an industrial nation, where the roots of liberalism may be deeply implanted.

Under the monarchy, liberalism was the creed of an educated minority. But under the Republic, it has received the unqualified support of a middle class now grown large, of a not inconsiderable part of the workers, and of the peasantry. Fascism has virtually disappeared. Monarchism has become a memory. Communism, still supported by many workers, has been isolated by the solidarity of the democratic parties. Italian liberalism can at last look forward to a future with confidence.

— 7 —

LIBERALISM IN GERMANY: AN UNFINISHED PATTERN

Weakness of German Liberalism. Liberalism in Germany during the nineteenth century was a plant of stunted growth. It did not become the all-penetrating element in the life and thought of the nation as it did in England, France, and America. Why? Not because the Germans are by nature averse to the liberal way of life. The explanation must be sought in their history, which created conditions and developed attitudes favorable to the authoritarian, rather than to the liberal, way of life.

Hindrances to Liberalism. Germany never experienced a liberal revolution. No "1688," no "1776," no "1789" took place, as in England, America, and France; hence, liberty and equality did not become cherished traditions among the Germans. During the seventeenth and eighteenth centuries, Germany, unlike England and France, was a much divided country. Local loyalties in the many "Germanies" of those centuries precluded the concentration of popular discontent that led to revolution in united England and in united France. When unity came to Germany belatedly in 1870, it was achieved under a leadership, notably that of Bismarck, that was hostile to liberalism. Largely for this reason national unity was identified in Germany with authoritarian government. Hence, the political structure of the new nation, the German Empire, was built according to an authoritarian, not a liberal, pattern.

Like national unity, the Industrial Revolution came belatedly to Germany about the middle of the nineteenth century, fully a century after that in England. Prior to this change Germany was overwhelmingly agricultural, almost medieval in its economy. Serfdom persisted in Prussia until 1810; and in the Hapsburg dominions until 1848. Because of this industrial backwardness there did not then exist in Germany, as in England and in France, a large and influential middle class that historically gave power and drive to the liberal movement.

In such a soil the plant of liberalism could not flower. It had no historic roots in popular strivings for freedom and equality. It had no powerful middle class determined to destroy the authoritarianism of the absolute state. Whenever a liberal movement did arise it was supported chiefly by the idealistic, educated elements, not by the broad masses of the people. As a consequence, German liberalism, whatever its success at the outset, soon suffered complete collapse. The princes of the German states continued to maintain their absolute rule.

Hegel. The philosopher of the authoritarian state was Georg Wilhelm Hegel (1770-1831), whose influence was as great in Germany as that of Locke in England, of Rousseau in France, and of Jefferson in America. Hegel's political philosophy rests upon the basic assumption that society constitutes the link that binds the individual citizen to the state; and that society consists of classes, each with its rights and duties. The individual is to be considered primarily as a member of a class; apart from it he has little significance. In the view of Hegel the state is the all-powerful, all-embracing organism that rules the community. It, not the people, is sovereign. But the state rules through the medium of a constitution requiring that all acts of the government be within the compass of law, not willful, autocratic acts of those in authority. There is only one limitation on the power of the state, according to Hegel, a limitation made by itself; namely, it cannot invade the realm of conscience, religion. It therefore must tolerate all faiths. (*See Reading No. 38.*)

Beginnings of Liberalism. Not until after 1815 did a liberal movement arise in Germany. The "geographical expression," called "Germany," then consisted of thirty-eight virtually independent states, nearly all of them absolute monarchies. Inspired by the ideas of the Enlightenment and by the German liberation movement against Napoleon, the rising generation dedicated itself to the creation of a united, liberal Germany. The movement attracted considerable attention, and roused general enthusiasm because of its militant opposition to the tyranny and narrowness of the ruling princes. It made considerable progress everywhere in Germany, especially in the two large states, Austria and Prussia.

Revolution of 1848. The year 1848 is an historic year in the history of liberalism. Inspired by the February Revolution in France, a revolutionary wave rolled eastward, engulfing almost every country in Western and Central Europe. Frightened monarchs yielded, and granted constitutions establishing some of the rudiments of the liberal state. For a time it appeared that liberalism was to be the wave of the future.

Especially important was the Revolution of 1848 in Germany. At first it made dramatic progress in Austria and in Prussia, the two states on which hinged everything political in Germany. Revolutionary uprisings in Vienna and in Berlin compelled the Austrian Emperor and the Prussian King to convene assemblies to draft constitutions.

Frankfort Assembly. As in Italy, the problem in Germany was to create a free, united nation. This became the objective of the Revolution of 1848. To attain this objective an Assembly was elected, representing all the German states, that met in Frankfort. Its purpose, like that of the Philadelphia Convention in America, was to adopt a constitution that would unite the various states into one nation. The Frankfort Assembly, famous in the annals of liberalism, issued a document, "Fundamental Rights of the German Nation," proclaiming liberal principles similar to those of the French Declaration of the Rights of Man. (*See Reading No. 39.*) In 1849 it adopted a democratic constitution establishing a federal union of the German states (except Austria), modeled in part on that of the United States. The union was to be monarchical, not republican in form, and the headship was offered to the King of Prussia as "Emperor."

Suppression of the Revolution. High were the hopes of the German liberals of 1848, and deep was to be their disappointment. The rulers recovered their courage, and turned with fury on the revolutionists. In Austria and in

Prussia they dismissed the assemblies that they had convened. Then, in 1850, King Frederick William IV of Prussia granted a constitution, one that was anything but liberal. It vested supreme power, not in the people, but in the king, aided by an assembly elected by a class system of voting weighted in favor of the propertied elements. This Prussian constitution remained in force until 1918.

Even more tragic was the fate of the Frankfort Assembly. The Prussian King disdainfully refused the position of "Emperor." He then determined to suppress that body and to nullify its work. The "Fundamental Rights of the German Nation" was repealed; the federal constitution was abolished; and the Assembly was suppressed by Prussian soldiers. The great effort to unite Germany on a liberal basis ended in complete failure.

The "unfilled revolution" resulted in a general reaction against liberalism. It became almost a "bad word" in Germany, implying ineptitude, failure, weakness, and chaos. Those seeking national unity now favored ideas and methods other than liberal to attain their aim. The failure of the Frankfort Assembly was to have momentous consequences for Germany and for the world.

Bismarck. With the rise of Count Otto von Bismarck (1815-1898) to power in Prussia the movement for German unity took a different direction. Hitherto, liberalism and nationalism had been political Siamese twins, in that one was joined to the other. Though it failed of its purpose, the Frankfort Assembly had succeeded in popularizing the idea of German unity. Bismarck realized that the unification of Germany lay in "the logic of history." However, unlike Cavour, he was determined to unite Germany outside of liberalism, even in opposition to it. According to Bismarck, Prussia was to compel the other German states, except Austria, to join a union formed and dominated by it. Therefore, Prussia had need of a powerful army, ready and able to fight all opponents, domestic and foreign, of such a union.

The Crisis of 1862. To prepare Prussia for its role, Bismarck, as Prime Minister, proposed an army budget in 1862. Parliament, in which the Liberals had a majority, refused to pass the budget. The government, in defiance of the constitution of 1850, then proceeded to levy and to collect taxes to be used for the new army. A bitter conflict raged between Parliament and Bismarck. In a famous speech Bismarck asserted his contempt for parliamentary methods. "Germany," he declared, "does not look to Prussia's liberalism, but to her power. . . . The great questions of the day are not to be decided by speeches and majority resolutions—therein lay the weakness of 1848 and 1849—but by iron and blood." Popular opinion supported Parliament but that did not deter Bismarck in his defiance of the constitution. And nothing happened to stop him. When Prussia triumphed over Austria in the Seven Weeks' War (1866), a wave of nationalist enthusiasm swept over Germany. Liberalism was all but forgotten, and the Prussian Parliament passed an act of indemnity legalizing Bismarck's unconstitutional acts.

Unification of Germany. German liberalism emerged from its trials in 1848 and in 1862, defeated, discouraged, and subdued. It was now prepared to accept whatever was given to it. A constitution, the author of which was Bismarck, was adopted in 1867 by the parliament of the federated northern states, known as the North German Confederation. After the great victory of Prussia over France in the Franco-Prussian War (1870-1871), Bismarck's constitution was accepted by the southern states. It then became the constitution of the united nation, the German Empire.

This constitution created a political system unlike any other then in existence. The German Empire was a federal union of twenty-five states, headed by the King of Prussia as German Emperor. Prussia was granted special privileges so important that it dominated the Empire; hence, the king, who was all but absolute in Prussia, indirectly exerted great power in the Empire. The Reichstag, elected by manhood suffrage, had the power to pass laws, which, however, had to have the consent of the Bundesrat, dominated by the rulers of the various states. Moreover, the Reichstag had no control of the ministry, which was appointed by and responsible to the Emperor. The federal constitution contained no Bill of Rights. Neither did it provide for the supremacy of the civil over the military power; the army was given so many special privileges that it became almost "a state within a state."

The Rechtstaat. It would be incorrect to describe the German Empire either as an autocratic or as a liberal state. Its constitution illustrated the contour of the German political mind, which harbored such obvious contradictions as authoritarianism and liberalism, hierarchical feudalism and social radicalism, and constitutional government without parliamentary supremacy. The German idea of the role of the state was expounded by a widely influential school of political science that advocated what was called the *Rechtstaat,* or juridical state. According to the *Rechtstaat,* the people were to be represented in an elected assembly. But the assembly was not to be an organ of the government with power to make laws for the nation, but a forum to air popular views. Its chief function was to bring the government expressions of popular opinion in order to enlighten it as to policies. The assembly might freely criticize the government, but could not overthrow it by a vote of "no confidence." Under no circumstances was the government to be subject to the will of shifting majorities.

What about civil liberty according to the *Rechtstaat*? The rights of the individual were to be defined and granted by the state itself; hence, he did not have, as under liberalism, natural rights as over against the state. Moreover, his rights depended on his status as a member of a class: worker, peasant, merchant, professional, or landowner. And it was the duty of the state to promote the welfare of every class in order to promote loyalty to the nation. Before the law, however, all citizens, irrespective of class, were equal. In these ways, according to the *Rechtstaat,* the liberty of the individual was made to harmonize with loyalty to the state and with national solidarity. Its upholders defined liberty as "the free, conscious and dutiful dedication of oneself to the whole, as it has been molded by history, state and nation." (*See Readings Nos. 40 and 41.*)

Though the German Empire could not be characterized as a liberal state it exhibited in some ways liberal contrasts to its authoritarian organization. In the sphere of thought and expression the nation enjoyed a high degree of intellectual freedom. No system of censorship existed; hence, liberty of speech, of the press, of teaching, and of authorship was generally maintained. German writers had free scope of inquiry and of publication. In the field of religion almost complete toleration prevailed.

The German Empire became the pioneer of social security legislation, today an integral part of the advanced stage of liberalism. Laissez faire, so influential in England and France, had no counterpart in Germany. Instead, Germany was motivated by the tradition of paternalism, whereby it was the duty of the state to advance the welfare of every class through protective legislation. During 1883-1889, long before the liberal nations, the Empire enacted laws giving benefits to insured workers, in cases of sickness, industrial accidents, old age, and invalidity. (*See Reading No. 42.*)

Middle Class, not Liberal. Contradiction followed contradiction in the unfinished pattern of German liberalism. The middle class, the protagonist of liberalism in Britain and France, played an entirely diffierent role in Germany. After unification Germany became a highly industrialized nation. A large, prosperous influential middle class appeared that loyally supported the authoritarian government of the Empire. Why? Again, historical circumstances give the explanation. In competing with their British rivals, long established in the world market, the German businessmen turned to the government for aid. And the government readily and generously aided them through protective tariffs, subsidies, special advantages in commercial treaties, and in many other ways. The business interests needed the protection and aid of the government not only against foreign competitors but also against domestic foes. Soon after the establishment of the Empire, the workers flocked to the banner of socialism. Fear of revolution and confiscation caused the middle class to turn to the government for protection. They opposed the liberalization of the constitution of the Empire, lest it result in giving power to the socialists, who might enact laws hostile to the business interests.

Because of the political timidity of the middle class the government encountered opposition chiefly among the socialist workers. In the Reichstag, the Social Democratic party, the largest socialist party in Europe, bitterly criticized the government and its policies. But opponents did not constitute an Opposition. Because there existed no ministerial responsibility every Chancellor, or Prime Minister, in the history of the Empire was identified with the conservative parties. Twice, during 1913, the Reichstag, backed by the socialist and radical parties, passed votes of "no confidence" in the government. The Ministry did not resign. From its creation in 1871 to its abolition in 1919 the structure of the German Empire remained virtually unchanged.

Democratic Liberalism. The defeat of Germany in the First World War led straight to the abolition of the Empire. Its successor, the Weimar Republic, was established in 1919 by a popularly elected constitutional convention. The Weimar constitution made Germany the very model of democratic liberalism. In form the government was a federal republic, headed by a popularly elected president. The principle of popular sovereignty was incorporated in the Reichstag, elected by universal suffrage, including women. It exercised supreme authority in the state through its power to pass laws and to control the ministry. The constitution contained an elaborate Bill of Rights which included the traditional rights of man; and, in addition, new rights, such as the right to work, to education, and to nationalize industries. Social legislation under the Republic was extended to include insurance against unemployment and a national eight-hour work day.

It would be hardly an exaggeration to describe the Weimar Republic as a liberal regime without liberals. A child of defeat, it was not wholeheartedly accepted by the people. Opposed to the Republic were powerful groups in German life, military, economic, and political, that hated it and all that it stood for. These groups appealed to the authoritarian traditions of the Germans who had had little experience in democratic government. That the Republic did not receive the solid support of the people became apparent when General Paul von Hindenburg was elected President in 1925, and again in 1931. President von Hindenburg, a Prussian army officer with no sympathy for popular rule, had little understanding of the nature of the liberal state over which he presided. When confronted by serious problems the parties in office, generally Social Democrats and Catholic Center, proved to be weak and inept. This aroused the contempt of a people accustomed to the decisive, strong rule of the Empire. Were a critical situation to arise the historic weakness of German liberalism would imperil the very existence of the Republic.

Fall of the Republic. Such a situation did arise when the Great Depression of 1929 hit Germany. Discontent, widespread and desperate, arose among the millions of ruined middle-class and of unemployed workers. To find a way out, the Germans instinctively turned to authoritarian parties, the Nazis on the right and the Communists on the left. Both were determined to destroy the Weimar Republic whose rootless liberalism would offer little resistance.

The elections of March, 1933, resulted in the third great crisis in the history of German liberalism. A large majority of the voters supported the parties hostile to the Republic: the Nazis, the Communists, and the Nationalists. The Nazis and their allies, the Nationalists, had a majority in the Reichstag. When Adolph Hitler, leader of the Nazis, demanded full power to establish a totalitarian dictatorship, he received the support of every party then in the Reichstag, except the Social Democrats. What followed was the swift destruction of the Republic and the establishment of the dictatorship of Hitler. As its birth was unexpected, the life of the Weimar Republic was short; and its death, sudden.

The Fascist system, established by the Nazi party, was a totalitarian dictatorship, the most comprehensive and the most despotic of all authoritarian governments. During its existence, from 1933 to 1945, every vestige of liberalism was wiped out in Germany.

Liberalism in Divided Germany. The Nazi system did not survive the defeat of Germany in the Second World War. It was completely destroyed, but with it was also destroyed the unity of Germany, attained after a century of heroic effort. The central and eastern parts fell under Communist rule, hence lost to liberalism. What was saved of Germany was the western part, established in 1949 as the independent German Federal Republic, with its capital at Bonn.

The constitution of the Republic, adopted by a popularly elected convention, established a system of government modeled largely on that of the Weimar Republic. In some respects it was even more emphatically liberal than the latter, notably in the protection of civil liberties.

In the mid-twentieth century the outlook for the survival of liberalism in the Republic was favorable. The historic enemies of German liberalism, Prussia, the Junker aristocracy, and the military caste, were all eliminated. Prussia was abolished. The Junkers were destroyed as a class through the confiscation of their estates in eastern Germany. The new army was made, definitely and specifically, subordinate to the civil authority. Konrad Adenauer, a truly liberal statesman and a strong, uncompromising, upholder of the regime, became Chancellor. The leading political parties, the Christian Democrats and the Social Democrats, with a large majority of the voters behind them, evinced unswerving loyalty to the government. Furthermore, the Republic consistently aligned itself with the Western nations in the world struggle against Communist totalitarianism. The Germany that had played so fateful a part in the history of liberalism was no more.

— 8 —

LIBERALISM IN AMERICA: FROM JEFFERSONIAN DEMOCRACY TO THE NEW DEAL

America, "Conceived in Liberty." America was born a liberal nation. It came into existence during the high noon of the Enlightenment when the libertarian ideas of the period found easy lodgment in the fresh soil of the New World. All the founders of America were liberals:

some more so, like Jefferson and Paine; others less so, like Hamilton and John Adams. All accepted the Declaration of Independence and the system of government established by the Constitution. Largely for this reason political conflicts in America have been between "conservatives," or liberals of the right, and "progressives," or liberals of the left. The former have sought to conserve the eighteenth-century ideas of individual freedom as an established tradition to be followed; and the latter have sought to reinterpret and to expand these ideas in the light of changing conditions. Revolutionary and reactionary parties, seeking to subvert the existing order, have had little influence in America.

The United States was created by a method, novel at the time, of a constitutional convention. This body adopted a written constitution establishing a new system of government for the newly-born nation; and the system was the outcome of the debates, discussions, and compromises by the delegates to the Philadelphia convention. To many then the birth of the new nation seemed an actual application of the theory of the social contract so widely held in the eighteenth century. The creation of a united nation through voluntary action, not through conquest, constituted a liberal innovation.

Another liberal innovation was the comprehensive Bill of Rights built into the constitution itself. Most of the state constitutions already had Bills of Rights, but fear was expressed that the central government might prove tyrannical. It became evident that the Constitution would not be ratified by the states unless such a Bill was attached to it. The first Ten Amendments, adopted in 1791, became the American Bill of Rights.

Still another liberal innovation was the safeguard erected against colonialism. Even before the adoption of the Constitution in 1788, the Northwest Ordinance of 1787 provided for the expansion of the country by voluntary, democratic methods. The Ordinance established in the Northwest Territory a system of government based on political, civil, and religious liberty. It forbade the introduction of slavery. In time the Territory was to be admitted as states in the Union "on an equal footing with the original States in all respects whatever." Annexation of territory without conquest, and the incorporation of a new population on the basis of equality with the old, created a liberal pattern of national expansion. (*See Reading No. 43.*)

Society in America. To develop a liberal society, so difficult in Europe, was comparatively easy in America. A frontier land, large in extent, sparsely inhabited, and rich in natural resources America did not—could not—reproduce the social order of Europe, derived from feudalism, with its privileges and discriminations. Unlike Europe America has had no entrenched aristocracy jealous of its privileged status; no fearful bourgeoisie guarding its property interests; no tenacious peasantry rooted in the soil; and no class-conscious proletariat resentful of its misery. From its very beginning the United States presented the unique opportunity of establishing in the New World a liberal society, one based on individual initiative and free from the privileges of an aristocracy, from the power of a military caste, and from the official creed of a national church. The United States emerged, according to *The Liberal Tradition in America* by Louis Hartz, "a nation built in the liberal image and yet without the feudalism that liberalism destroyed."

Fly in the Liberal Ointment. There was, however, an ugly fly in the ointment of American liberalism, Negro slavery. The fathers of the Constitution did not abolish the institution. Believing that slavery was on the way out, they inserted a provision forbidding the importation of Negro slaves after 1808. In the Constitutional Convention a struggle took place over representation, resulting in a compromise that indirectly recognized slavery. The Constitution provided for a system of representation in the House of Representatives, counting the "Free Persons" and "three fifths of all other Persons." But the situation in regard to slavery changed radically as a result of the invention of the cotton gin. So important did cotton become economically that slavery became a vested interest in the Southern states.

Bourgeois Liberalism. Because the Constitution had established America as a liberal state no struggle took place, as in Europe, between liberals and reactionaries. What might be described as bourgeois liberalism was advocated by the Federalist party, the great spokesman of which was Alexander Hamilton (1757-1804). According to the Federalists, government should be in the hands of the propertied, educated elements, "the better kind of people." The non-propertied workers were, in their view, irrational, turbulent, and envious; hence, unfit to participate in the government of the nation. The Federalists, in power until 1800, put the country on a firm basis. Congress adopted Hamilton's recommendations: to secure the credit of the new nation by its assumption of all the war debts; to create financial stability by establishing a national bank and a monetary system; and to encourage domestic industry by a protective tariff.

Jeffersonian Democracy. Opposed to the Federalists were the Republicans, later known as the Democrats. The founder and great spokesman of the Democratic party was Thomas Jefferson (1743-1826), who was elected President in 1800. Democratic liberalism in America has its primal source in the ideas of this philosopher-statesman. Jeffersonian democracy comprehended free, public, secular education; laissez faire on the theory that the best government was the one that governed least; manhood suffrage, to be realized not by abolishing property qualifications but by giving full opportunity to acquire it and thus to qualify; separation of church and state; and especially freedom of speech and of the press. (*See Reading No. 44.*) The Jeffersonian principle of equal rights to all and special privileges to none became the rallying cry of America.

Democratic Liberalism. The next great advance of American liberalism took place during the Jacksonian period. The Industrial Revolution in the North and the settlement of the West resulted in the creation of a social order uniquely American. Property could be acquired by anyone through free enterprise in business or through the acquisition of free land in the West. Freedom of enterprise was not an abstract principle but a living experience to many Americans. Capitalism, a bourgeois institution in Europe, became a popular one in America where individualism, self-reliance, initiative, and ambition had a free field. Largely for this reason, laissez faire, a bourgeois policy in Europe, became in America a popular ideal.

The immense resources of the country, waiting to be exploited, and the large, free market created by the Union offered endless opportunities for business enterprise. Many rose from the ranks to become property owners.

As a result of the loose, ill-defined class structure, liberalism in America advanced to the democratic stage earlier than in Europe. Manhood suffrage was virtually established in the North and West during the 1830's. Government by the "people" now meant that the voice of the common man was heard in the land.

Another aspect of democratic liberalism, popular education, made rapid headway. By the middle of the nineteenth century, free, public, elementary schools were universal in the North and the West. Steps were also taken to establish free higher education through state universities and city colleges. The Morrill Act of 1862 recognized the principle of higher education as a public responsibility, and granted lands to the states to be used as an endowment for the support of education to advance industry and agriculture. Many of the state universities and land-grant colleges sprang from this Act. Something unique in the history of education was created in America: an open corridor from the lowest to the highest grades, free, public, and secular. And the corridor was made increasingly wider to accommodate the growing numbers seeking higher education.

The right freely to change nationality, by emigration from one country to another, has been regarded as a liberal tenet. America proclaimed this right by its open door immigration policy. During the nineteenth century great waves of immigrants flowed from Europe to America. The problem was how to assimilate, how to "Americanize" the heterogeneous mass of foreigners. Failure to do so would have resulted in a divided America consisting of congealed, mutually hostile nationalities, each with its special traditions, language, and culture. To a remarkable degree America succeeded in solving this problem, through free, public education, an easy method of acquiring citizenship, and especially the many opportunities to rise on the economic ladder.

In the process of Americanization a new concept of liberal nationalism was developed. It was to appeal to a common future rather than to that of a common past. Englishmen and Frenchmen, because of their long history, have known who and what they are. Not so Americans, whose past was short but whose future was boundless. The new, as well as the old, Americans were inspired by the appeal of a common future to build a democratic civilization as a model for the world. It was brought home to the immigrants that they came to America voluntarily seeking a better and freer life; and that though they came in masses they were admitted as individuals. In becoming a citizen an immigrant was integrated into the life and destiny of the nation that he chose to be his new fatherland. This concept of nationalism generated a spirit of unity in America that in Europe was associated with a common historic past, a common race, and a common faith.

Slavery, a Danger to Unity. National unity, however, was threatened by the institution of slavery. Until the Negro was integrated as a free and equal citizen in America the bright hopes of democratic liberalism could not be fully realized. The problem of slavery became more insistent as the slave states of the South became more differentiated from the free states of the North. Cotton culture being the foundation of its economy and Negro labor regarded as essential to it, the South was determined to maintain slavery. America was now a house divided against itself, half slave, half free. (*See Reading No. 45.*) Despite compromise after compromise the conflict between them became inevitable.

It came to a head with the election in 1860 of the Republican, Abraham Lincoln, as President. When the Civil War broke out, Lincoln clearly realized that in the preservation of the Union lay the only possibility of maintaining America as the great exemplar of democratic liberalism. Throughout the War he consistently upheld this view, to which he gave immortal expression in his Gettysburg Address. (*See Reading No. 46.*) With the defeat of the South came a new birth of freedom in America. Slavery was abolished by the Thirteenth Amendment; and equal citizenship was granted to all irrespective of "race, color, or previous condition of servitude" by the Fourteenth and Fifteenth Amendments. The Negro now became a free man and a citizen. (*See Reading No. 47.*)

Wealth against Commonwealth. The phenomenal economic development of America after the Civil War posed new problems for the democratic liberalism. National wealth increased by leaps and bounds, but the various elements of the population shared in it unequally. Immense fortunes were made by great capitalists who exerted a powerful influence on political life. The concentration of industry into trusts drove many small producers to the wall. Private corporations got control of much of the public domain. Many independent farmers either sold their holdings or were reduced to being tenants. In the crowded cities lived masses of workers, ill paid and ill housed. Bitter antagonism developed between small and big business, between farmers and the financial interests, and between employers and workers. (*See Reading No. 48.*)

How did democratic liberalism meet the new issue of "wealth against commonwealth"? Radical political movements demanded the curbing of the power of great corporations. To protect small businessmen and farmers Congress passed the Interstate Commerce Act (1887), regulating railway rates and prohibiting the railway companies from "giving undue advantages to large shippers"; and the Sherman Anti-Trust Act (1890), prohibiting combinations in restraint of trade. These measures constituted the first steps in the recognition by the government of its responsibility for the welfare of the "small man," thereby preparing the way for the new liberalism.

Chief among the political groups that espoused the new liberalism was the Populist party, organized in 1892. It demanded both political and economic reforms: popular election of Senators; the Initiative and Referendum; a graduated income tax; government ownership of railroads; the curbing of the trusts; and especially the free coinage of silver and the curbing of the "Money Power," or "Wall Street." A significant change took place in American politics during the Presidential election of 1896. The Democratic party fell under the control of the progressive element that succeeded in nominating William J. Bryan on what was virtually a Populist platform.

Though the Democratic party was defeated, it became identified with radical policies in the interest of small businessmen, farmers, and workers. A new liberalism was now in the making.

Progressivism. As the new liberalism gathered force it became known as the Progressive movement. It influenced both political parties and inspired the organization of new, and more radical, parties. Corrupt politics and "Big Business" became the special object of its hostility. In the tradition of American liberty, Progressivism demanded the participation of the individual in matters political by the elimination of bossism; and in matters economic by demanding the dissolution, or at least the curbing, of the trusts. It was influential in the enactment of such measures as the Pure Food and Drugs Act (1906), forbidding adulteration of food and of drugs; and laws favoring the conservation of forest lands. A decision of the Supreme Court in Northern Securities case (1904) struck at monopoly by forbidding the consolidation of several large railroads.

Progressivism was marching on. It scored a great triumph in the Presidential election of 1912. The Democratic candidate, Woodrow Wilson (1856-1924), was elected on an advanced platform that became known as the "New Freedom." Equally significant was the appearance during the campaign of the Progressive party, whose candidate, the ex-Republican Theodore Roosevelt, received a larger vote than did the Republican candidate, William H. Taft. The Socialist candidate, Eugene V. Debs, rolled up a surprising vote, about 900,000. The outcome of the election was a great triumph for those parties that favored progressivism.

The "New Freedom." During the Presidency of Woodrow Wilson the Progressive era of American politics definitely emerged. The following measures were notable examples of the new tendency: the Federal Reserve Act (1913), reforming the banking and currency systems; the Trade Commission Act (1914), preventing unfair competition in business; the Clayton Act (1914), making more effective the laws against monopoly, and declaring that labor unions were not monopolies. Three amendments to the Constitution became part of the new liberal pattern: the Sixteenth (1913), empowering Congress to pass an income tax; the Seventeenth (1913), establishing popular election of Senators; and the Nineteenth (1920), extending the suffrage to women.

The liberalism of the "New Freedom" found expression in foreign as well as in domestic affairs. When, in 1917, America entered the war on the side of the Allies, it abandoned its traditional isolationism, convinced that its way of life could survive only in a world "made safe for democracy." The international outlook of the new liberalism was superbly expressed by President Wilson. Largely because of his influence the League of Nations, the first world organization, was created in 1920, with the object of settling disputes between nations by peaceful methods. Though the League was rejected by America, and went out of existence during the Second World War, it established a precedent for a world organization to maintain peace. This precedent was followed, in 1945, when the United Nations was organized with the full support of America.

Rise of Social Liberalism. During the period between the two World Wars liberalism in America, as in Europe, became markedly social in outlook. Its efforts were directed toward increasing the regulatory power of government over economic life. What precipitated this tendency was the Great Depression of 1929. The ruin of many in every walk of life resulted in the widespread conviction that government intervention in economic life was vital to the welfare of the people and to the security of the nation. Popular discontent resulted in the triumph of the Democratic party in 1932, when its candidate, Franklin D. Roosevelt (1882-1945), was elected President. His election was as notable in the history of American liberalism as that of Jefferson in 1800, of Jackson in 1824, and of Lincoln in 1860. His administration marked the beginning of the decisive advance of American liberalism to the social stage that was to culminate in the Welfare state. In a notable message President Roosevelt formulated what he called an "economic Bill of Rights" guaranteeing the right of the worker to a satisfactory standard of living; the right of the farmer to fair prices for his products; the right of every citizen to medical care; and the right of everyone to protection against the economic hazards of life. (*See Reading No. 49.*)

During 1933-1938 a series of radical reforms repudiated laissez faire, and gave a distinctively social orientation to American liberalism. These reforms became known as the New Deal, the American version of the Welfare State, the essential character of which was government regulation of economic life with the object of allocating the national income so as to provide a minimum of well-being for everyone able and willing to work.

To realize this objective, social security laws provided for old age pensions and for unemployment insurance. The National Wages and Hours Act established a minimum wage and a maxium work week for those employed in interstate commerce. The Agricultural Adjustment Act gave government aid to farmers. The National Labor Relations Act guaranteed to labor unions the right of collective bargaining. The Tennessee Valley Authority (TVA) established government ownership of water power in the Valley. The Securities and Exchange Act provided protection for investors. Something like a social revolution was effected in America by the New Deal.

So popular was the New Deal that Roosevelt was elected President for four consecutive terms. On his death, in 1945, he was succeeded by Vice-President Harry S. Truman, who was elected President in 1948. A change of government took place when the Republican, Dwight D. Eisenhower, was elected President in 1952 and again in 1956. This shift in party control was not followed by a repudiation of the New Deal. The Republicans accepted, even extended, it in some ways. America was now definitely committed to the Welfare State.

The Negro Problem. The new liberalism of social rights brought a new emphasis on the old liberalism of individual rights. It focused attention on that element of the population that had benefited least from America's progress, the Negro. After the Civil War the Negro was free but not equal. In the South he became a second-class citizen: deprived of his vote, his civil rights flouted, legally segregated in public places, and limited economically to menial occupations. Elsewhere in America he was kept in a lowly status by discriminatory practices in employment, in education, in housing, and in many other ways. The Negroes constituted a caste of outcasts in the America that boasted of giving equal rights to all and special privileges to none.

This condition of the Negro became what has been called America's "dilemma." The contradiction became glaring when America entered the First World War "to make the world safe for democracy." And even more so when, in the Second World War, it waged war against Nazi Germany that proclaimed racial discrimination as its fundamental principle.

After the war America determined to come to grips with the Negro problem. During the decade 1945-55, the status of the Negro underwent an immense improvement. Negroes were increasingly permitted to vote in the South. Lynching virtually ceased. Segregation was abolished in the armed forces. Some of the states passed laws forbidding discrimination in employment because of race, creed, or national origin. By far the most important step in the movement to resolve America's "dilemma" was the unanimous decision of the Supreme Court, delivered on May 17, 1954. It declared unconstitutional all laws establishing segregation in the public schools on the ground that such measures deprived Negroes "of the equal protection of the laws guaranteed by the Fourteenth Amendment." (*See Reading No. 50.*) This famous decision was greeted throughout the world as a great vindication of the liberal principle of equality.

America, World Defender of Liberalism. Liberalism has been on the march in America since the day of the Declaration of Independence. Until the twentieth century, however, its accomplishments were largely confined to America itself. But the two World Wars profoundly changed this situation. History thrust America forward as the most powerful and most determined champion of the democratic way of life, first against the militarism of Imperial Germany, and then against the totalitarian dictatorship of fascism. Since then the hopes of liberals everywhere rest on America as the leader of the free world in its ceaseless struggle against the totalitarian dictatorship of communism.

— 9 —

THE LASTING VALUES OF LIBERALISM

At the beginning of the twentieth century the outlook for liberalism appeared bright. Only two autocracies were left in Europe, Russia and Turkey, and both were threatened by revolution. In the semi-liberal German Empire the rapid growth of the Social Democratic party inspired hope for the peaceful transformation of Germany into a democratic state. France was finally established as a democratic republic. In the New World, America was a firmly united democracy. When Canada was established as a self-governing "Dominion," traditional imperialism was undermined. Even in backward Asia, liberalism advanced when Japan was organized as a semi-liberal state. Because of these notable advances it was generally assumed that liberalism was destined to encompass the entire world.

Then came the two World Wars, both within one generation, 1914-1945. So great was the destruction of life and property, and so fearful the methods of warfare that many feared that the progress of mankind had come to an end. During the same period the world was shaken by two world revolutions, communism and fascism, the effects of which were far greater than those of any previous revolution. Both fascism and communism repudiated liberalism in theory and in practice, and in any and all forms. The system of totalitarian dictatorship established by communism in Russia and by fascism in Italy and in Germany, constituted a complete negation of liberalism.

The defeat of Nazi Germany and Fascist Italy in the Second World War eliminated fascism as a threat to liberalism. At the same time it made more ominous the threat of Communist Russia which succeeded in gaining control of about one-third of the world.

Never before had liberalism been challenged by an enemy so powerful, so resourceful, so implacable. In the great struggle that followed, liberalism asserted its principles with a new emphasis, with a re-awakened ardor, and with greater militancy, especially in America, Britain, and France. These nations were convinced that liberalism had made lasting contributions to the welfare of mankind, and they had to be preserved at whatever cost. What have been these contributions?

First and foremost has been the maintenance of the civil rights of the individual. In a more vital sense than ever before it has now become clear that without liberty of opinion and of faith, man's creative impulses become sterilized; that without equality, civil and political, no sense of human dignity can be generated; and that without the constitutional protection of persons and of property no security is possible for anyone. The recognition of the autonomy of the individual is the very keystone of liberalism. Civil rights have become a more cherished heritage now that they have been totally suppressed in Communist lands.

Liberalism has contributed much to the solution of the problem of power as exercised by the state. It has taken to heart Lord Acton's famous dictum, "All power tends to corrupt, and absolute power corrupts absolutely." No absolute power is given to anyone in the liberal scheme of government; its acts are subject to judicial review. Neither is power exercised without responsibility to the people, who freely grant or withhold power to govern at periodic elections.

Absolute rule was given a death blow by liberalism when it made opposition to the government a legitimate, even a necessary, function. Opposition is expressed not only by minority political parties but also by numerous and varied organizations that aim to change the policies of the government by constitutional methods. When those in power, the majority, agree to share existence with those out of power, the minority, a change of rulers becomes easy and peaceful. This contribution of liberalism to the art of government has brought stability with progress, has promoted national unity, and has assured the continuity of the constitutional state.

Liberalism devised a rational method for settling differences between opposing interests. This method channels conflicts of all kinds—social, economic, religious, racial and ideological—into political issues to be settled peacefully at the polls. Open warfare is thereby avoided. Once a conflict becomes a political issue it is evaluated in terms of the public interest. That distinctively liberal concept, the "general welfare," takes precedence in public opinion over special interests. The outcome generally is a compromise, accepted with good or bad grace by both sides. Liberalism has provided the best machinery yet available for reconciling conflicting interests.

Peaceful methods of settling domestic problems have inspired liberals to devise similar methods to settle conflicts among nations. Liberals have been in the forefront in the movement to abolish war as an instrument of national policy. To this end they have sought to establish a world organization dedicated to the preservation of universal peace. Largely through the efforts of liberals was founded first, the League of Nations, and later, its successor, the United Nations. In the past, liberalism was the great force that succeeded in abolishing slavery and serfdom. Now it is the great force that is striving to abolish war.

The liberal spirit has, in modern times, found expression in all of man's interests. But nowhere more so than in the field of government, now extended to include so many of man's activities. The liberal state may be considered as the masterpiece of political man, an institution dedicated to preserving and enlarging human freedom in all ways. Never until now has the destiny of mankind been weighed on a political scale. And that scale is the liberal state.

Part II

READINGS

— Reading No. 1 —

HOBHOUSE: LIBERALISM AND THE INDIVIDUAL[1]

In his book, Liberalism, *the noted English sociologist, Leonard Trelawney Hobhouse (1864-1929), gives an excellent analysis of liberalism in general and of English liberalism in particular. The following excerpt states what, in his view, constitutes the foundation of liberalism.*

✓ ✓ ✓

Liberalism is the belief that society can safely be founded on this self-directing power of personality, that it is only on this foundation that a true community can be built, and that so established its foundations are so deep and so wide that there is no limit that we can place to the extent of the building. Liberty then becomes not so much a right of the individual as a necessity of society. It rests not on the claim of A to be let alone by B, but on the duty of B to treat A as a rational being. . . . The rule of liberty is just the application of the rational method. It is the opening of the door to the appeal of reason, of imagination, of social feeling; and except through the response to this appeal there is no assured progress of society.

[1] L. T. Hobhouse, *Liberalism* (New York, 1913), p. 123.

— Reading No. 2 —

SOCRATES: INTELLECTUAL FREEDOM[2]

In his teachings, in his life, and in his death, Socrates (c. 470-399 B.C.*) was the supreme exemplar, in ancient times, of intellectual freedom. A martyr to the cause of intellectual freedom, Socrates yet had no notion of what is now called the "natural right" of every individual, as over against the state, to life, liberty, and the pursuit of happiness. He stoutly maintained the right of the state to execute him, even though he was unjustly condemned.*

The first excerpt is from the Apology; *the second, from* Crito.

✓ ✓ ✓

I

. . . Men of Athens, I honor and love you; but I shall obey God rather than you, and while I have life and strength I shall never cease from the practice and teaching of philosophy, exhorting anyone whom I meet after my manner, and convincing him, saying: O my friend why do you care so much about laying up the greatest amount of money and honor and reputation, and so little about wisdom and truth and the greatest improvement of the soul, which you never regard or heed at all? . . . This is my teaching, and if this is the doctrine which corrupts the youth, my influence is ruinous indeed. . . . Wherefore, O men of Athens, I say to you, . . . either acquit me or not; but whatever you do, know that I shall never alter my ways, not even if I have to die many times. . . .

[2] *Dialogues of Plato,* with Introduction by the translator, Benjamin Jowett (New York, 1899), pp. 24, 44.

II

. . . For I am and always have been one of those natures who must be guided by reason, whatever the reason may be which upon reflection appears to me to be the best; and now that this fortune has come upon me, I cannot put away the reasons which I have before given: the principles which I have hitherto honored and revered I still honor, and unless we can find other and better principles on the instant, I am certain not to agree with you; no, not even if the power of the multitude could inflict many more imprisonments, confiscations, deaths, frightening us like children with hobgoblin terrors. . . .

— Reading No. 3 —

ABÉLARD: YEA AND NAY[3]

Peter Abélard (1079-1142) was the enfant terrible *of the Catholic theologians of medieval France. In his book,* Sic et Non (Yea and Nay), *he sought to clarify Christian dogmas by a novel method of persistent questioning. In his book he states 158 problems in theology, and then balances authorities, pro and con, leaving the reader to find his own solution. This method, Abélard claimed, would clear away the seeming obscurities and contradictions in the writings of the Church Fathers. Moreover, it would sharpen the wits of the readers. The book shocked the theologians, and Abélard was made to suffer for his temerity.*

The following excerpt gives some of the problems raised in Yea and Nay.

Should human faith be based on reason, or no?
Is God one, or no?
Is God a substance, or no?
Does the first Psalm refer to Christ, or no?
Is sin pleasing to God, or no?
Is God the author of evil, or no?
Is God all-powerful, or no?
Can God be resisted, or no?
Has God free will, or no?
Was the first man persuaded to sin by the devil, or no?
Was Adam saved, or no?
Did all the apostles have wives except John, or no?

[3] James Harvey Robinson (ed.), *Readings in European History* (New York, 1904), I, 449-452.

Are the flesh and blood of Christ in very truth and essence present in the sacrament of the altar, or no?
Do we sometimes sin unwillingly, or no?
Does God punish the same sin both here and in the future, or no?
Is it worse to sin openly than secretly, or no?

— Reading No. 4 —

ERASMUS: THE PHILOSOPHY OF CHRIST[4]

The Dutch Renaissance scholar and theologian, Desiderius Erasmus (1465-1536), was the greatest of all Christian humanists. He aimed to reform the Catholic church from within by satirizing many of the religious beliefs and practices of his time. Erasmus achieved an international reputation as a classical scholar, which was greatly enhanced by his translation of the New Testament from Greek to Latin.

The following excerpt from his book, Enchiridion, *explains what Erasmus called the "pure fountain of the gospel."*

✓ ✓ ✓

And yet there is no man but he ought to use a good life, to the which Christ would that the way should be plain and open for every man, and not by inexplicable crooks of disputations, not able to be resolved, but by a true and sincere faith and charity not feigned, whom hope doth follow which is never ashamed. . . .

. . . Therefore, in mine opinion, the best were that some both well learned men and good of living should have this office assigned and put unto them, to make a collection and to gather the sum of Christ's philosophy out of the pure fountain of the gospel and the epistles and most approved interpreters, and so plainly that yet it might be clerkly and erudite, and so briefly that it might also be plain. Those things which concern faith or belief,

[4] Desiderius Erasmus, *Enchiridion* (London, 1905), pp. 5, 10.

let them be contained in a few articles. Those also that appertain to the manner of living let them be shewed and taught in few words, and that after such fashion that they may perceive the yoke of Christ to be pleasant and easy, and not grievous and painful.

— Reading No. 5 —

DESCARTES: THE METHODS OF REASONING[5]

The Frenchman, René Descartes (1596-1650), inaugurated what has been called the Cartesian Revolution in philosophy by applying the logical method of mathematics to philosophy. In his book, Discourse on Method *(1637), Descartes rejected scholasticism, and established the principles of modern rationalism.*

The following excerpt explains the four principles of Descartes' method of reasoning.

✓ ✓ ✓

The First was never to accept anything for true which I did not clearly know to be such; that is to say, carefully to avoid precipitancy and prejudice, and to comprise nothing more in my judgment than what was presented to my mind so clearly and distinctly as to exclude all ground of doubt. *The Second,* to divide each of the difficulties under examination into as many parts as possible, and as might be necessary for its adequate solution. *The Third,* to conduct my thoughts in such order that, by commencing with objects the simplest and easiest to know, I might ascend by little and little, and, as it were, step by step, to the knowledge of the more complex; assigning in thought a certain order even to those objects which in their own nature do not stand in a relation of antecedence and sequence. At the *Last,* in every case to make enumerations so complete, and reviews so general, that I might be assured that nothing was omitted.

[5] John Veitch, *The Method, Meditation and Philosophy of Descartes* (New York, 1901), p. 161.

— Reading No. 6 —

MILTON: CENSORSHIP[6]

The famous tract, Areopagitica *(1644), written by John Milton (1608-1674), is a classic document in the history of freedom of thought. It was occasioned by the law, passed by Parliament, creating a body of censors with power to grant licenses to print.*

In the following excerpt Milton makes a highly eloquent plea for freedom to publish.

I deny not, but that it is of greatest concernment in the church and commonwealth, to have a vigilant eye how books demean themselves, as well as men; and thereafter to confine, imprison, and do sharpest justice on them as malefactors; for books are not absolutely dead things, but do contain a progeny of life in them to be as active as that soul was whose progeny they are; nay, they do preserve as in a vial the purest efficacy and extraction of that living intellect that bred them. I know they are as lively, and as vigorously productive, as those fabulous dragon's teeth: and being sown up and down, may chance to spring up armed men. And yet, on the other hand, unless wariness be used, as good almost kill a man as kill a good book: who kills a man kills a reasonable creature, God's image; but he who destroys a good book, kills reason itself, kills the image of God, as it were, in the eye. Many a man lives a burthen to the earth; but a good book is the precious lifeblood of a master-spirit, em-

[6] John Milton, *Areopagitica and other Prose Writings,* ed. William Haller (New York, 1927), pp. 8-9.

balmed and treasured up on purpose to a life beyond life. . . .

We should be wary, therefore, what persecution we raise against the living labours of public men, how we spill that seasoned life of man, preserved and stored up in books; since we see a kind of homicide may be thus committed, sometimes a martyrdom; and if it extend to the whole impression, a kind of massacre, whereof the execution ends not in the slaying of an elemental life, but strikes at the ethereal and fifth essence, the breath of reason itself, slays an immortality rather than a life.

— Reading No. 7 —

CONDORCET: THE MEANING OF PROGRESS[7]

Marie Jean Nicolas Caritat, Marquis de Condorcet (1743-1794), was the one prominent philosophe *who lived to become active in the French Revolution. Though not one of the Girondins he became identified with their policies. During the Reign of Terror, Condorcet was proscribed but he cheated the guillotine by committing suicide. His most famous book,* Sketch for a Historical Picture of the Progress of the Human Mind *(1795), was written while in hiding from the Terror. This "last will and testament of the Eighteenth Century" was the first book to treat with explicit fullness the idea of progress.*

In the following excerpts Condorcet gives his optimistic views of the future of mankind.

✓ ✓ ✓

The aim of the book that I have undertaken to write, and what it will prove, is that man by using reason and facts will attain perfection. Nature has set no limits to the perfection of the human faculties. The perfectibility of mankind is truly indefinite; and the progress of this perfectibility, henceforth to be free of all hindrances, will last as long as the globe on which nature has placed us. Doubtless this progress will be more or less rapid, but it will never retrograde, at least as long as the globe occupies its present place in the system of the universe; and unless

[7] Marquis de Condorcet, *Esquisse d'un Tableau historique des progrès de l'esprit humain* (Paris, 1829), pp. 7-8, 15, 247-248.

the general laws that govern this system bring to pass a universal cataclysm, or such changes as will prevent man from maintaining his existence, from using his faculties, and from finding his needed resources. . . .

Since the period when alphabetical writing flourished in Greece the history of mankind has been linked to the condition of man of our time in the most enlightened countries of Europe by an unbroken chain of facts and observations. The picture of the march and progress of the human mind is now revealed as being truly historical. Philosophy no longer has to guess, no longer has to advance hypothetical theories. It now suffices to assemble and to arrange the facts, and to show the truths that arise from their connection and from their totality. . . .

If man can predict with almost complete certainty those phenomena whose laws he knows; and if, when he does not know these laws, he can, on the basis of his experience in the past, predict future events with assurance why then should it be regarded as chimerical to trace with a fair degree of accuracy the picture of man's future on the basis of his history? The sole foundations for belief in the natural sciences is the principle that universal laws, known or unknown, which regulate the universe are necessary and constant. Why then should this principle be less true for the development of the intellectual and moral faculties of man than it is for the other operations of nature? Finally, since beliefs, based on past experience under like conditions, constitute the only rule according to which the wisest men act, why then forbid the philosopher to support his beliefs on the same foundations, as long as he does not attribute to them a certainty not warranted by the number, the constancy, and the accuracy of his observations. . . .

— Reading No. 8 —

LOCKE: RELIGION, NO CONCERN OF THE GOVERNMENT[8]

John Locke (1632-1704) has been considered as the fountainhead of English political and religious liberalism. His version of the social contract was generally accepted both in England and America during the eighteenth century. In his Letter Concerning Toleration *(1689) he expressed views on religious toleration far in advance of his time, though he did not favor extending toleration to Catholics and to atheists.*

The following excerpts give Locke's view of religion as a private matter.

✓ ✓ ✓

. . . All the power of civil government relates only to men's civil interests, is confined to the care of things in this world, and hath nothing to do with the world to come.

Let us now consider what a church is. A church then I take to be a voluntary society of men, joining themselves together of their own accord, in order to the public worshipping of God, in such manner as they judge acceptable to him, and effectual to the salvation of their souls.

I say it is a free and voluntary society. . . . No man by nature is bound unto any particular church or sect, but everyone joins himself voluntarily to that society in which he believes he has found that profession and worship which is truly acceptable to God. . . . No member of a religious society can be tied with any other bonds but

[8] John Locke, *Letter Concerning Toleration* (London, 1800), pp. 19-21, 85-87, 102-104.

what proceed from the certain expectation of eternal life. . . .

. . . Speculative opinions, therefore, and *articles of faith* as they are called, which are required only to be believed, cannot be imposed on any Church by the law of the land. . . .

Further, the magistrate ought not to forbid the preaching or professing of any speculative opinions in any Church, because they have no manner of relation to the civil rights of the subjects. . . . But the business of laws is not to provide for the truth of opinions, but for the safety and security of the commonwealth, and of every particular man's goods and person. . . .

Again: That church can have no right to be tolerated by the magistrate, which is constituted upon such a bottom, that all those who enter it, do thereby *ipso facto,* deliver themselves up to the protection and service of another prince. For by this means the magistrate would give way to the settling of a foreign jurisdiction in his own country, and suffer his own people to be listed, as it were, for soldiers against his own government. . . .

Lastly, Those are not at all to be tolerated who deny the being of God. Promises, covenants, and oaths, which are the bonds of human society, can have no hold upon an atheist. The taking away of God, though but even in thought, dissolves all. Besides also, those that by their atheism undermine and destroy all religion, can have no pretence of religion whereupon to challenge the privilege of a toleration. . . .

— Reading No. 9 —

VOLTAIRE: REASON AND TOLERANCE[9]

François Marie Arouet de Voltaire (1694-1778), French writer and philosopher, became the leading champion of religious and intellectual freedom of the Enlightenment. He satirized with great wit the intolerant practices of his day. Voltaire's Treatise on Tolerance *(1673) was inspired by his vindication of Jean Calas, a Protestant falsely convicted and executed on the charge of having murdered his son to prevent his conversion to Catholicism.*

In the following excerpts Voltaire denounces the evils of intolerance.

. . . The great means to reduce the number of fanatics, if any remain, is to submit that disease of the mind to the treatment of reason, which slowly, but infallibly, enlightens men. Reason is gentle and humane. It inspires liberality, suppresses discord, and strengthens virtue; it has more power to make obedience to the laws attractive than force has to compel it. And shall we take no account of the ridicule that attaches today to the enthusiasm of these good people? Ridicule is a strong barrier to the extravagance of all sectarians. . . .

The supposed right of intolerance is absurd and barbaric. It is the right of the tiger; nay, it is far worse, for tigers do but tear in order to have food, while we rend each other for paragraphs. . . .

Do I propose, then, that every citizen shall be free to

[9] Voltaire, *Treatise on Tolerance,* trans. Joseph McCabe (New York, 1912), pp. 27-28, 30-31, 83.

follow his own reason, and believe whatever this enlightened or deluded reason shall dictate to him? Certainly, provided he does not disturb the public order. It does not depend on man to believe or not to believe; but it depends on him to respect the usages of his country. . . .

One does not need great art and skillful eloquence to prove that Christians ought to tolerate each other—nay, even to regard all men as brothers. Why, you say, is the Turk, the Chinese, or the Jew my brother? Assuredly; are we not all children of the same father, creatures of the same God?

— Reading No. 10 —

CONDORCET: A NATIONAL SYSTEM OF EDUCATION[10]

As Chairman of a Committee on Education appointed by the Legislative Assembly during the French Revolution, Condorcet issued his "Report on the General Organization of Knowledge" (1792). It is based on his belief in popular education as essential to human progress. The Report is a great document in the history of liberal education.

The following excerpt stresses education in the promotion of general welfare.

✓ ✓ ✓

To offer to all individuals of the human race the means of providing for their needs, of assuring their welfare, of knowing and exercising their rights, of understanding and fulfilling their obligations. To assure each one the facility of perfecting his skill, of rendering himself capable of the social functions to which he has the right to be called, of developing to the fullest extent those talents with which nature has endowed him; and thereby to establish among all citizens an actual equality, thus rendering real the political equality recognized by the law. This should be the first aim of any national education; and, from such a point of view, this education is for the government an obligation of justice.

To direct the teaching in such a manner that the per-

[10] Thomas C. Mendenhall and Others (eds.), *The Quest for a Principle of Authority in Europe, 1715-Present* (New York, 1948), p. 64. Reprinted by permission of Henry Holt and Company, Inc.

fecting of the industries shall increase the pleasures of the generality of the citizens and the welfares of those who devote themselves to them, that a greater number of men shall be capable of exercising the functions necessary to society, and that the ever-increasing progress of enlightenment shall provide an inexhaustible source of help in our needs, of remedies for our ills, of means of individual happiness and of general prosperity. In short, to cultivate in each generation the physical, intellectual, and moral faculties, and thereby contribute to the general and gradual improvement of the human race—which should be the final aim of every social institution. This likewise should be the object of education, and it is for the government a duty imposed on it by the common interest of society, by that of all mankind.

As the first requisite of all education is that only the truth be taught, all institutions established by the government should be as free as possible from all political control, and, since this independence cannot be absolute, it results from the same principle that they must depend only on the Assembly of the Representatives of the People. . . .

Above the primary schools, education ceases to be absolutely general. But we have felt that the double objective of assuring the country all the talents that could serve it, and of not depriving any individual of the advantage of developing those with which he has been endowed would be attained, if the children who show the most aptitude in a given grade of instruction should be chosen to enter the next higher; and maintained at the expense of the national treasury; they would be called National Scholars. According to the plan proposed by the committee, 3850 children, or thereabouts, would receive a sum sufficient for their maintenance. Of these, 1000 would attend the institutes and 600 the lyceums. About 400 would come out each year to take up useful employments in society or to devote themselves to the sciences. Never in any country has the government opened for the poorer classes a more abundant source of prosperity and learning; never has it used more powerful means to maintain the natural equality of men. Not alone will the study of the sciences be encouraged, but also that modest industry, which seeks only to make easier the admittance to a laborious profession, will not be neglected. As it is desirable that there be also rewards for diligence, for love of work, and for integrity, even when not accompanied by brilliant qualities, the government will provide for other National Scholars their apprenticeship in industries of general utility. . . .

— Reading No. 11 —

ADAM SMITH: ADVANTAGES OF FREE ENTERPRISE[11]

The Scotsman, Adam Smith (1723-1790), has been recognized as the outstanding economic thinker of the Enlightenment. His famous book, Wealth of Nations *(1776), was the primal source of the ideas of the classical school of economics. The principle of free trade and of laissez faire, advocated by Adam Smith, served greatly to destroy the mercantilist system, and to inaugurate the system of free enterprise.*

The following excerpts explain what Adam Smith called the "system of natural liberty."

✓ ✓ ✓

All systems either of preference or restraint, therefore, being thus completely taken away, the obvious and simple system of natural liberty establishes itself of its own accord. Every man, as long as he does not violate the laws of justice, is left perfectly free to pursue his own interest his own way, and to bring both his industry and capital into competition with those of any other man, or order of men. The sovereign is completely discharged from a duty, in the attempting to perform which he must always be exposed to innumerable delusions, and for the proper performance of which no human wisdom or knowledge could ever be sufficient; the duty of superintending the industry of private people, and of directing

[11] Adam Smith, *An Inquiry into the Nature and Causes of the Wealth of Nations,* ed. E. Cannan (London, 1930), II, pp. 184-185; I, p. 421.

it toward the employments most suitable to the interest of the society. According to the system of natural liberty, the sovereign has only three duties to attend to; three duties of great importance, indeed, but plain and intelligible to common understandings: first, the duty of protecting the society from the violence and invasion of other independent societies; secondly, the duty of protecting, as far as possible, every member of the society from the injustice or oppression of every other member of it, or the duty of establishing an exact administration of justice; and thirdly, the duty of erecting and maintaining certain public works and certain public institutions, which it can never be for the interest of any individual, or small number of individuals, to erect and maintain; because the profit could never repay the expence to any individual or small number of individuals, though it may frequently do much more than repay it to a great society.

. . . As every individual, therefore, endeavors as much as he can both to employ his capital in the support of domestic industry; . . . and by directing that industry in such a manner as its produce may be of the greatest value, he intends only his own gain, and he is in this, as in many other cases, led by an invisible hand to promote an end which was no part of his intention. Nor is it always the worse for the society that it was no part of it. By pursuing his own interest he frequently promotes that of the society more effectually than when he really intends to promote it. I have never known much good done by those who affected to trade for the public good. It is an affectation, indeed, not very common among merchants, and very few words need be employed in dissuading them from it.

What is the species of domestic industry which his capital can employ, and of which the produce is likely to be of the greatest value, every individual, it is evident, can, in his local situation, judge much better than any statesman or lawgiver can do for him. The statesman who should attempt to direct private people in what manner they ought to employ their capitals would not only load himself with a most unnecessary attention, but assume an authority which could safely be trusted, not only to no single person, but to no council or senate whatever, and which would nowhere be so dangerous as in the hands of a man who had folly and presumption enough to fancy himself fit to exercise it.

To give the monopoly of the home market to the produce of domestic industry, in any particular art or manufacture, is in some measure to direct private people in what manner they ought to employ their capitals, and must, in almost all cases, be either a useless or a hurtful regulation. If the produce of domestic can be brought there as cheap as that of foreign industry, the regulation is evidently useless. If it cannot, it must generally be hurtful. It is the maxim of every prudent master of a family never to make at home what it will cost him more to make than to buy.

— Reading No. 12 —

LOCKE: GOVERNMENT BY THE CONSENT OF THE GOVERNED[12]

Locke's views on government became the fountainhead of English political liberalism. He wrote Of Civil Government *(1690) in defense of the Revolution of 1688. In this book he expounds his famous doctrine that no government is legitimate unless it has the consent of the governed, a doctrine accepted by liberals everywhere and at all times.*

The following excerpts give Locke's views of the origin of government, of its chief functions, and of the right of revolution.

✓ ✓ ✓

Men being, as has been said, by nature all free, equal, and independent, no one can be put out of this estate and subjected to the political power of another without his own consent, which is done by agreeing with other men, to join and unite into a community for their comfortable, safe, and peaceable living, one amongst another, in a secure enjoyment of their properties, and a greater security against any that are not of it. This any number of men may do, because it injures not the freedom of the rest; they are left, as they were, in the liberty of the state of Nature. When any number of men have so consented to make one community or government, they are thereby presently incorporated, and make one body politic, wherein the majority have a right to act and conclude the rest.

[12] John Locke, *Of Civil Government* (New York, 1924), pp. 164-165, 219, 228-229.

For, when any number of men have, by the consent of every individual, made a community, they have thereby made that community one body, with a power to act as one body, which is only by the will and determination of the majority. For that which acts any community, being only the consent of the individuals of it, and it being one body, must move one way, it is necessary the body should move that way whither the greater force carries it, which is the consent of the majority, or else it is impossible it should act or continue one body, one community, which the consent of every individual that united into it agreed that it should; and so every one is bound by that consent to be concluded by the majority. And therefore we see that in assemblies empowered to act by positive laws where no number is set by that positive law which empowers them, the act of the majority passes for the act of the whole, and of course determines as having, by the law of Nature and reason, the power of the whole. . . .

Wherever law ends, tyranny begins, if the law be transgressed to another's harm; and whosoever in authority exceeds the power given him by the law, and makes use of the force he has under his command to compass that upon the subject which the law allows not, ceases in that to be a magistrate, and acting without authority may be opposed, as any other man who by force invades the right of another.

. . . For since it can never be supposed to be the will of society that the legislative should have a power to destroy that which every one designs to secure by entering into society, and for which the people submitted themselves to legislators of their own making: whenever the legislators endeavor to take away and destroy the property of the people, or to reduce them to slavery under arbitrary power, they put themselves into a state of war with the people, who are thereupon absolved from any farther obedience, and are left to the common refuge which God hath provided for all men against force and violence. Whensoever, therefore, the legislative shall transgress this fundamental rule of society, . . . it devolves to the people, who have a right to resume their original liberty, and by the establishment of a new legislature (such as they shall think fit) provide for their own safety and security, which is the end for which they are in society. What I have said here concerning the legislative in general holds true also concerning the supreme executor, . . . when he goes about to set up his own arbitrary will as the law of society.

— Reading No. 13 —

MONTESQUIEU: SEPARATION OF THE POWERS OF GOVERNMENT[13]

Charles Louis de Secondat, Baron de la Brède et de la Montesquieu (1689-1775), the political philosopher of eighteenth-century France, came from a family of the judicial nobility. He devoted his life to the study of political institutions, and became world famous on the appearance of his book, The Spirit of Laws *(1748). Though an ardent lover of freedom Montesquieu may be described as a moderate in his political views.*

In the following excerpt he states his famous formula for the preservation of political liberty.

✓ ✓ ✓

In every government there are three sorts of power: the legislative; the executive in respect to things dependent on the law of nations; and the executive in regard to matters that depend on the civil law.

By virtue of the first, the prince or magistrate enacts temporary or perpetual laws, and amends or abrogates those that have been already enacted. By the second, he makes peace or war, sends or receives embassies, establishes the public security, and provides against invasions. By the third, he punishes criminals, or determines the disputes that arise between individuals. The latter we shall call the judiciary power, and the other simply the executive power of the state.

[13] Montesquieu, *The Spirit of Laws,* trans. Thomas Nugent (New York, 1900), I, 182-183.

The political liberty of the subject is a tranquility of mind arising from the opinion each person has of his safety. In order to have this liberty, it is requisite the government be so constituted as one man need not be afraid of another.

When the legislative and executive powers are united in the same person, or in the same body of magistrates, there can be no liberty, because apprehensions may arise lest the same monarch or senate should enact tyrannical laws, to execute them in a tyrannical manner.

Again, there is no liberty, if the judiciary power be not separated from the legislative and executive. Were it joined with the legislative, the life and liberty of the subject would be exposed to arbitrary control; for the judge would be then the legislator. Were it joined to the executive power, the judge might behave with violence and oppression.

There would be an end of everything, were the same man or the same body, whether of the nobles or of the people, to exercise those three powers: that of enacting laws, that of executing the public resolutions, and of trying the causes of individuals. . . .

— Reading No. 14 —

ROUSSEAU: INTERPRETATION OF THE SOCIAL CONTRACT[14]

Jean-Jacques Rousseau (1712-1778) was one of the major philosophes of eighteenth-century France. His Social Contract *(1762) is one of the greatest books on political philosophy written in modern times. It proclaimed the theory of popular sovereignty which profoundly influenced the French Revolution.*

In the following excerpts Rousseau explains the origin and nature of the social contract.

✓ ✓ ✓

To find a form of association which may defend and protect with the whole force of the community the person and property of every associate, and by means of which each, coalescing with all, may nevertheless obey only himself, and remain as free as before. Such is the fundamental problem of which the social contract furnishes the solution. . . .

In short, each giving himself to all, gives himself to nobody; and as there is not one associate over whom we do not acquire the same rights which we concede to him over ourselves, we gain the equivalent of all that we lose, and more power to preserve what we have. . . .

Forthwith, instead of the individual personalities of all the contracting parties, this act of association produces a moral and collective body, which is composed of as many members as the assembly has voices, and which

[14] Jean-Jacques Rousseau, *The Social Contract,* trans. Henry J. Tozer (London, 1924), pp. 109-111, 113, 114, 119, 121, 123. Reprinted by permission of George Allen and Unwin, London.

receives from this same act its unity, its common self (*moi*), its life, and its will. This public person, which is thus formed by the union of all the individual members . . . is called by its members *State* when it is passive, *sovereign* when it is active, *power* when it is compared to similar bodies. With regard to the associates they take collectively the name of *people*. . . .

Besides the preceding, we might add to the acquisitions of the civil state moral freedom which alone renders man truly master of himself; for the impulse of mere appetite is slavery, while obedience to a self-prescribed law is liberty. . . .

Now, the sovereign, being formed only of the individuals that compose it, neither has nor can have any interest contrary to theirs; consequently the sovereign power needs no guarantee towards its subjects, because it is impossible that the body should wish to injure all its members; and we shall see hereafter that it can injure no one as an individual. The sovereign, for the simple reason that it is so, is always everything that it ought to be. . . .

In order, then, that the social pact may not be a vain formula it tacitly includes this engagement, which can alone give force to the others,—that whoever refuses to obey the general will shall be constrained to do so by the whole body; which means nothing else than that he shall be forced to be free; . . .

I say, then, that sovereignty, being nothing but the exercise of the general will, can never be alienated, and that the sovereign power, which is only a collective being, can be represented by itself alone; power indeed can be transmitted but not will. . . .

For the same reason that sovereignty is inalienable it is indivisible; for the will is either general, or it is not; it is either that of the body of the people, or that of only a portion. . . .

It follows from what precedes that the general will is always right and always tends to the public advantage; but it does not follow that the resolutions of the people have always the same rectitude. Men always desire their own good, but do not always discern it; the people are never corrupted, though often deceived, and it is only then that they seem to will what is evil.

— Reading No. 15 —

THE ENGLISH BILL OF RIGHTS[15]

James II, a Catholic, became King of England in 1685. He had two objectives: to be an absolute ruler and to restore the Catholic church. In pursuance of these objectives James defied Parliament by suspending the operation of the laws against those who were not members of the established Church of England. The King's actions roused widespread fear in England. In 1688, Parliament declared the throne "vacant," and proclaimed the Netherlander, William, and his wife, Mary, King and Queen of England. This "Bloodless Revolution" definitely established the supremacy of Parliament over the king. It became part of the constitution by the adoption, in 1689, of the Bill of Rights, which follows.

Whereas the said late King James II having abdicated the government, and the throne being thereby vacant, his Highness the prince of Orange . . . (by the advice of the Lords spiritual and temporal, and divers principal persons of the Commons) . . . being now assembled in a full and free representative of this nation, taking into their most serious consideration the best means for attaining the ends aforesaid, do in the first place (as their ancestors in like case have usually done), for the vindicating and asserting their ancient rights and liberties, declare:

1. That the pretended power of suspending laws, or the execution of laws, by regal authority, without consent of Parliament, is illegal.

2. That the pretended power of dispensing with laws,

[15] R. P. Stearns (ed.), *Pageant of Europe* (New York, 1948), pp. 235-237.

or the execution of laws, by regal authority, as it has been assumed and exercised of late, is illegal.

3. That the commission for erecting the late Court of Commissioners for Ecclesiastical Causes, and all other commissions and courts of like nature, are illegal and pernicious.

4. That levying money for or to the use of the crown, by pretence of prerogative, without grant of Parliament, for longer time, or in other manner than the same is or shall be granted, is illegal.

5. That it is the right of the subjects to petition the king, and all commitments and prosecutions for such petitioning are illegal.

6. That the raising or keeping a standing army within the kingdom in time of peace, unless it be with consent of Parliament, is against law.

7. That the subjects which are Protestants may have arms for their defence suitable to their conditions, and as allowed by law.

8. That election of members of Parliament ought to be free.

9. That the freedom of speech, and debates or proceedings in Parliament, ought not to be impeached or questioned in any court or place out of Parliament.

10. That excessive bail ought not to be required, nor excessive fines imposed, nor cruel and unusual punishments inflicted.

11. That jurors ought to be duly impaneled and returned, and jurors which pass upon men in trials for high treason ought to be freeholders.

12. That all grants and promises of fines and forfeitures of particular persons before conviction are illegal and void.

13. And that for redress of all grievances, and for the amending, strengthening, and preserving of the laws, Parliament ought to be held frequently.

And they do claim, demand, and insist upon all and singular the premises, as their undoubted rights and liberties; and that no declarations, judgments, doings, or proceedings, to the prejudice of the people in any of the said premises, ought in any wise to be drawn hereafter into consequence or example. . . .

— Reading No. 16 —

DECLARATION OF INDEPENDENCE

On July 4, 1776 the Declaration of Independence, written by Thomas Jefferson, was adopted by the Continental Congress. The following first two paragraphs expound the principles of political liberalism, derived largely from the views of Locke.

✓ ✓ ✓

When in the Course of human events, it becomes necessary for one people to dissolve the political bands which have connected them with another, and to assume among the powers of the earth, the separate and equal station to which the Laws of Nature and of Nature's God entitle them, a decent respect to the opinions of mankind requires that they should declare the causes which impel them to the separation.

We hold these truths to be self-evident, that all men are created equal, that they are endowed by their Creator with certain unalienable Rights, that among these are Life, Liberty and the pursuit of Happiness.——That to secure these rights, Governments are instituted among Men, deriving their just powers from the consent of the governed, —— That whenever any Form of Government becomes destructive of these ends, it is the Right of the People to alter or abolish it, and to institute new Government, laying its foundation on such principles and organizing its powers in such form, as to them shall seem most likely to effect their Safety and Happiness. Prudence, indeed, will dictate that Governments long established should not be changed for light and transient causes; and accordingly all experience hath shewn, that mankind are more disposed to suffer, while evils are sufferable, than to right themselves by abolishing the forms to which they are accustomed. But when a long train of abuses and usurpations, pursuing invariably the same Object evinces a design to reduce them under absolute Despotism, it is their right, it is their duty, to throw off such Government, and to provide new Guards for their future security.——Such has been the patient sufferance of these Colonies; and such is now the necessity which constrains them to alter their former Systems of Government. The history of the present King of Great Britain is a history of repeated injuries and usurpations, all having in direct object the establishment of an absolute Tyranny over these States. To prove this, let Facts be submitted to a candid world.

— Reading No. 17 —

THE AMERICAN BILL OF RIGHTS

The first ten Amendments, known as the Bill of Rights, became part of the American Constitution on December 15, 1791.

1. Congress shall make no law respecting an establishment of religion, or prohibiting the free exercise thereof; or abridging the freedom of speech, or of the press; or the right of the people peaceably to assemble, and to petition the government for a redress of grievances.
2. A well-regulated militia being necessary to the security of a free state, the right of the people to keep and bear arms shall not be infringed.
3. No soldier shall, in time of peace, be quartered in any house, without the consent of the owner; nor in time of war, but in a manner to be prescribed by law.
4. The right of the people to be secure in their persons, houses, papers, and effects, against unreasonable searches and seizures, shall not be violated; and no warrants shall issue, but upon probable cause, supported by oath or affirmation, and particularly describing the place to be searched, and the persons or things to be seized.
5. No person shall be held to answer for a capital or other infamous crime unless on a presentment or indictment of a Grand Jury, except in cases arising in the land or naval forces, or in the militia, when in actual service, in time of war or public danger; nor shall any person be subject, for the same offense, to be twice put in jeopardy of life or limb; nor shall be compelled, in any criminal case, to be a witness against himself; nor be deprived of life,

liberty, or property, without due process of law; nor shall private property be taken for public use, without just compensation.

6. In all criminal prosecutions, the accused shall enjoy the right to a speedy and public trial, by an impartial jury of the state and district wherein the crime shall have been committed, which district shall have been previously ascertained by law, and to be informed of the nature and cause of the accusation; to be confronted with the witnesses against him; to have compulsory process for obtaining witnesses in his favor, and to have the assistance of counsel for his defense.

7. In suits at common law, where the value in controversy shall exceed twenty dollars, the right of trial by jury shall be preserved, and no fact tried by a jury shall be otherwise re-examined in any court of the United States than according to the rules of the common law.

8. Excessive bail shall not be required, nor excessive fines imposed, nor cruel and unusual punishments inflicted.

9. The enumeration in the Constitution of certain rights shall not be construed to deny or disparage others retained by the people.

10. The powers not delegated to the United States by the Constitution, nor prohibited by it to the states, are reserved to the states respectively, or to the people.

— Reading No. 18 —

THE DECLARATION OF THE RIGHTS OF MAN AND OF THE CITIZEN[16]

On August 27, 1789 the Constituent Assembly adopted this famous Declaration. It formulated the underlying principles that were to guide this body in renovating France.

✓ ✓ ✓

The representatives of the people of France, formed into a National Assembly, considering that ignorance, neglect, or contempt of human rights, are the sole causes of public misfortunes and corruptions of government, have resolved to set forth in a solemn declaration, these natural, imprescriptible, and inalienable rights: that this declaration being constantly present to the minds of the members of the body social, they may be forever kept attentive to their rights and duties; that the acts of the legislative and executive powers of government, being capable of being every moment compared with the end of political institutions, may be more respected; and also, that the future claims of the citizens, being directed by simple and incontestable principles, may always tend to the maintenance of the Constitution, and the general happiness.

For these reasons, the National Assembly doth recognize and declare, in the presence of the Supreme Being, and

[16] Thomas C. Mendenhall and Others (eds.), *The Quest for a Principle of Authority in Europe, 1715-Present* (New York, 1948), pp. 60-61. Reprinted by permission of Henry Holt and Company, Inc.

with the hope of His blessing and favor, the following *sacred* rights of men and citizens:

I. Men are born, and always continue, free and equal in respect of their rights. Civil distinctions, therefore, can be founded only on public utility.

II. The end of all political associations is the preservation of the natural and imprescriptible rights of man; and these rights are liberty, property, security, and resistance of oppression.

III. The nation is essentially the source of all sovereignty; nor can any individual, or any body of men, be entitled to any authority which is not expressly derived from it.

IV. Political liberty consists in the power of doing whatever does not injure another. The exercise of the natural rights of every man, has no other limits than those which are necessary to secure to every *other* man the free exercise of the same rights; and these limits are determinable only by law.

V. The law ought to prohibit only actions hurtful to society. What is not prohibited by the law, should not be hindered; nor should anyone be compelled to that which the law does not require.

VI. The law is an expression of the will of the community. All citizens have a right to concur, either personally, or by their representatives, in its formation. It should be the same to all, whether it protects or punishes; and all being equal in its sight, are equally eligible to all honors, places, and employments, according to their different abilities, without any other distinction than that created by their virtues and talents.

VII. No man should be accused, arrested, or held in confinement, except in cases determined by the law, and according to the forms which it has prescribed.

VIII. The law ought to impose no other penalties but such as are absolutely and evidently necessary; and no one ought to be punished, but in virtue of a law promulgated before the offense, and legally applied.

IX. Every man being presumed innocent till he has been convicted, whenever his detention becomes indispensable, all rigor to him, more than is necessary to secure his person, ought to be provided against by the law.

X. No man ought to be molested on account of his opinions, not even on account of his *religious* opinions, provided his avowal of them does not disturb the public order established by the law.

XI. The unrestrained communication of thoughts and opinions being one of the most precious rights of man, every citizen may speak, write, and publish freely, provided he is responsible for the abuse of this liberty, in cases determined by the law.

XII. A public force being necessary to give security to the rights of men and of citizens, that force is instituted for the benefit of the community and not for the particular benefit of the persons to whom it is intrusted.

XIII. A common contribution being necessary for the support of the public force, and for defraying the other expenses of government, it ought to be divided equally among the members of the community, according to their abilities.

XIV. Every citizen has a right, either by himself or his representative, to a free voice in determining the necessity of public contributions, the appropriation of them, and their amount, mode of assessment, and duration.

XV. Every community has a right to demand of all its agents an account of their conduct.

XVI. Every community in which a separation of powers and a security of rights is not provided for, wants a constitution.

XVII. The right to property being inviolable and sacred, no one ought to be deprived of it, except in cases of evident public necessity, legally ascertained, and on condition of a previous just indemnity.

— Reading No. 19 —

RICARDO: ON LABOR AND ON FREE TRADE[17]

David Ricardo (1772-1823), British economist, formulated the fundamental principles of the classical school in his book, The Principles of Political Economy and Taxation *(1817). Ricardo's view of labor as a commodity for long acted as a deterrent to state intervention on behalf of the workers. His famous "law of rent" undermined the economic position of the landed aristocracy, and led to the establishment of free trade.*

The following excerpts present Ricardo's views on these two problems.

✓ ✓ ✓

Labour, like all other things which are purchased and sold, and which may be increased or diminished in quantity, has its natural and its market price. The natural price of labour is that price which is necessary to enable the labourers, one with another, to subsist and to perpetuate their race, without either increase or diminution.

The power of the labourer to support himself, and the family which may be necessary to keep up the number of labourers, does not depend on the quantity of money which he may receive for wages but on the quantity of food, necessaries, and conveniences become essential to him from habit which that money will purchase. The natural price of labour, therefore, depends on the price of the food, necessaries, and conveniences required for the support of the labourer and his family. . . .

[17] David Ricardo, *The Principles of Political Economy and Taxation* (New York, 1926), pp. 52, 70, 53, 81.

The necessity which the labourer would be under of paying an increased price for such necessaries would oblige him to demand more wages; and whatever increases wages, necessarily reduces profits. . . .

It is when the market price of labour exceeds its natural price that the condition of the labourer is flourishing and happy, that he has it in his power to command a greater proportion of the necessaries and enjoyments of life, and therefore to rear a healthy and numerous family. When, however, by the encouragement which high wages give to the increase of population, the number of labourers is increased, wages again fall to their natural price, and indeed from a reaction sometimes fall below it. . . .

Under a system of perfectly free commerce, each country naturally devotes its capital and labour to such employments as are most beneficial to each. This pursuit of individual advantage is admirably connected with the universal good of the whole. By stimulating industry, by rewarding ingenuity, and by using efficaciously the peculiar powers bestowed by nature, it distributes labour most effectively and most economically: while, by increasing the general mass of productions, it diffuses general benefits, and binds together, by one common tie of interest and intercourse, the universal society of nations throughout the civilized world. It is this principle which determines that wine shall be made in France and Portugal, that corn shall be grown in America and Poland, and that hardware and other goods shall be manufactured in England. . . .

— Reading No. 20 —

MALTHUS: SUBSISTENCE AND POPULATION[18]

Thomas Robert Malthus (1766-1834), the pioneer student of demography, or the science of population, was first a clergyman, then a professor of history and political economy. His book, An Essay on the Principle of Population *(1798), created a sensation. It was a pessimistic reply to the optimistic views of those who believed that mankind was destined to achieve a happy future.*

The following excerpts present what became known as "Malthusianism."

✓ ✓ ✓

That population has this constant tendency to increase beyond the means of subsistence, and that it is kept to its necessary level . . . will sufficiently appear from a review of the different states of society in which man has existed. . . .

It may safely be pronounced, therefore, that population, when unchecked, goes on doubling itself every twenty-five years, or increases in a geometrical ratio. . . .

It may be fairly pronounced, therefore, that considering the present average state of the earth, the means of subsistence, under circumstances the most favorable to human industry, could not possibly be made to increase faster than in an arithmetical ratio.

The ultimate check to population appears then to be a want of food, arising necessarily from the different ratios according to which population and food increase. But this

[18] T. R. Malthus, *An Essay on the Principle of Population* (New York, 1927), I., 6-10, 12-13, 314-315.

ultimate check is never the immediate check, except in cases of actual famine.

The immediate check may be stated to consist in all those customs, and all those diseases, which seem to be generated by a scarcity of the means of subsistence; and all those causes, independent of this scarcity, whether of a moral or physical nature, which tend prematurely to weaken and destroy the human frame.

These checks to population, which are constantly operating with more or less force in every society, and keep down the number to the level of the means of subsistence, may be classed under two general heads—the preventive and the positive checks.

The preventive check, as far as it is voluntary, is peculiar to man, and arises from that distinctive superiority in his reasoning faculties which enables him to calculate distant consequences. The checks to the indefinite increase of plants and irrational animals are all either positive, or, if preventive, involuntary. But man cannot look around him and see the distress which frequently presses upon those who have large families; he cannot contemplate his present possessions or earnings, which he now nearly consumes himself, and calculate the amount of each share, when with very little addition they must be divided, perhaps, among seven or eight, without feeling a doubt whether, if he follow the bent of his inclinations, he may be able to support the offspring which he will probably bring into the world. In a state of equality, if such can exist, this would be the simple question. In the present state of society other considerations occur. Will he not lower his rank in life, and be obliged to give up in great measure his former habits? Does any mode of employment present itself by which he may reasonably hope to maintain a family? Will he not at any rate subject himself to greater difficulties, and more severe labour, than in his single state? Will he not be unable to transmit to his children the same advantages of education and improvement that he had himself possessed? Does he even feel secure that, should he have a large family, his utmost exertions can save them from rags and squalid poverty, and their consequent degradation in the community? And may he not be reduced to the grating necessity of forfeiting his inde-

pendence, and of being obliged to the spar
Charity for support?

Must it not then be acknowledged by an a
examiner of the histories of mankind, that, in ever
and in every state in which man has existed or does n
exist,

The increase of population is necessarily limited by the means of subsistence:

Population invariably increases when the means of subsistence increase, unless prevented by powerful and obvious checks:

These checks, and the checks which keep the population down to the level of the means of subsistence, are moral restraint, vice, and misery?

ng No. 21 —

SURVIVAL OF THE ECONOMICALLY FIT[19]

Herbert Spencer (1820-1903), British sociologist and scientist, upheld the extreme views of classical liberalism. A believer in social Darwinism, he was convinced that the fittest would survive in the competitive economic struggle. And that meant, according to Spencer, the progress of civilization.

In the following excerpt Spencer strongly opposes government intervention on behalf of the poor.

In common with its other assumptions of secondary offices, the assumption by a government of the office of Reliever-general to the poor, is necessarily forbidden by the principle that a government cannot rightly do anything more than protect. In demanding from a citizen contributions for the mitigation of distress-contributions not needed for the due administration of men's rights—the state is, as we have seen, reversing its function, and diminishing that liberty to exercise the faculties which it was instituted to maintain. Possibly, . . . some will assert that by satisfying the wants of the pauper, a government is in reality extending his liberty to exercise his faculties. . . . But this statement of the case implies a confounding of two widely-different things. To enforce the fundamental law—to take care that every man has freedom to do all that he wills, provided he infringes not the equal freedom of any other man—this is the special

[19] Herbert Spencer, *Social Statics* (London, 1851), pp. 311, 322-323.

purpose for which the civil power exists. Now insuring to each the right to pursue within the specified limits the objects of his desires without let or hindrance, is quite a separate thing from insuring him satisfaction. . . .

Pervading all nature we may see at work a stern discipline, which is a little cruel that it may be very kind. That state of universal warfare maintained throughout the lower creation, to the great perplexity of many worthy people, is at bottom the most merciful provision which the circumstances admit of. . . . The poverty of the incapable, the distresses that come upon the imprudent, the starvation of the idle, and those shoulderings aside of the weak by the strong, which leave so many "in shallows and in miseries," are the decrees of a large, far-seeing benevolence. It seems hard that an unskilfulness which with all its efforts he cannot overcome, should entail hunger upon the artizan. It seems hard that a labourer incapacitated by sickness from competing with his stronger fellows, should have to bear the resulting privations. It seems hard that widows and orphans should be left to struggle for life or death. Nevertheless, when regarded not separately, but in connection with the interests of universal humanity, these harsh fatalities are seen to be full of the highest beneficence—the same beneficence which brings to early graves the children of diseased parents, and singles out the low-spirited, the intemperate, and the debilitated as the victims of an epidemic. . . .

— Reading No. 22 —

DEWEY: INDIVIDUALISM UNDER A SOCIALIZED ECONOMY[20]

John Dewey (1859-1952), American philosopher and educator, exercised a profound influence in shaping liberal thought in America. He was also deeply interested in political, social, and economic problems; his point of view was that of an advanced social liberal.

In the following excerpt, Dewey shows the inadequacy of laissez faire liberalism under modern conditions.

✓ ✓ ✓

Since liberation of the capacities of individuals for free, self-initiated expression is an essential part of the creed of liberalism, liberalism that is sincere must will the means that condition the achieving of its ends. Regimentation of material and mechanical forces is the only way by which the mass of individuals can be released from regimentation and consequent suppression of their cultural possibilities. . . . The notion that organized social control of economic forces lies outside the historic path of liberalism shows that liberalism is still impeded by remnants of its earlier laissez faire phase, with its opposition of society and the individual. . . . Earlier liberalism regarded the separate and competing economic action of individuals as the means to social well-being as the end. We must reverse the perspective and see that socialized economy is the means of free individual development as the end.

[20] John Dewey, *Liberalism and Social Action* (New York, 1935), p. 90.

— Reading No. 23 —

UNIVERSAL DECLARATION OF HUMAN RIGHTS[21]

On December 10, 1948, the General Assembly of the United Nations adopted and proclaimed the Universal Declaration of Human Rights. For the first time in history an international body, representing fifty-eight nations, issued such a Declaration. The Soviet bloc, Saudi Arabia, and the Union of South Africa abstained from voting.

The following extracts constitute its chief provisions.

✓ ✓ ✓

THE GENERAL ASSEMBLY

proclaims

THIS UNIVERSAL DECLARATION OF HUMAN RIGHTS as a common standard of achievement for all peoples and all nations, to the end that every individual and every organ of society, keeping this Declaration constantly in mind, shall strive by teaching and education to promote respect for these rights and freedoms and by progressive measures, national and international, to secure their universal and effective recognition and observance, both among the peoples of Member States themselves and among the peoples of territories under their jurisdiction.

All human beings are born free and equal in dignity and rights. They are endowed with reason and conscience and should act towards one another in a spirit of brotherhood.

Everyone is entitled to all the rights and freedoms set forth in this Declaration, without distinction of any kind,

[21] From the text published by the Department of Public Information of the United Nations.

such as race, colour, sex, language, religion, political or other opinion, national or social origin, property, birth or other status. Furthermore, no distinction shall be made on the basis of the political, jurisdictional or international status of the country or territory to which a person belongs, whether it be independent, trust, non-self-governing or under any other limitation of sovereignty.

Everyone has the right to life, liberty and security of person. . . .

No one shall be subjected to torture or to cruel, inhuman or degrading treatment or punishment. . . .

All are equal before the law and are entitled without any discrimination to equal protection of the law. All are entitled to equal protection against any discrimination in violation of this Declaration and against any incitement to such discrimination. . . .

No one shall be subjected to arbitrary arrest, detention or exile. . . .

Everyone charged with a penal offence has the right to be presumed innocent until proved guilty according to law in a public trial at which he has had all the guarantees necessary for his defence. . . .

No one shall be subjected to arbitrary interference with his privacy, family, home, or correspondence, nor to attacks upon his honor and reputation. Everyone has the right to the protection of the law against such interference or attacks.

Everyone has the right to freedom of movement and residence within the borders of each state.

Everyone has the right to leave any country, including his own, and to return to his country.

Everyone has the right to seek and to enjoy in other countries asylum from persecution. . . .

Everyone has the right to a nationality.

No one shall be arbitrarily deprived of his nationality nor denied the right to change his nationality.

Men and women of full age, without any limitation due to race, nationality or religion, have the right to marry and to found a family. They are entitled to equal rights as to marriage, during marriage and at its dissolution.

Marriage shall be entered into only with the free and full consent of the intending spouses.

The family is the natural and fundamental group unit of society and is entitled to protection by society and the State. . . .

Everyone has the right to freedom of thought, conscience and religion; this right includes freedom to change his religion or belief, and freedom, either alone or in community with others and in public or private, to manifest his religion or belief in teaching, practice, worship and observance.

Everyone has the right to freedom of opinion and expression; this right includes freedom to hold opinions without interference and to seek, receive and impart information and ideas through any media and regardless of frontiers.

Everyone has the right to freedom of peaceful assembly and association.

Everyone has the right to take part in the government of his country, directly or through freely chosen representatives.

Everyone has the right of equal access to public service in his country.

The will of the people shall be the basis of the authority of government; this will shall be expressed in periodic and genuine elections which shall be by universal and equal suffrage and shall be held by secret vote or by equivalent free voting procedures.

Everyone, as a member of society, has the right to social security and is entitled to realisation, through national effort and international co-operation and in accordance with the organisation and resources of each State, of the economic, social and cultural rights indispensable for his dignity and the free development of his personality.

Everyone has the right to work, to free choice of employment, to just and favourable conditions of work and to protection against unemployment.

Everyone, without any discrimination, has the right to equal pay for equal work.

Everyone who works has the right to just and favourable remuneration insuring for himself and his family an existence worthy of human dignity, and supplemented, if necessary, by other means of social protection.

Everyone has the right to form and to join trade unions for the protection of his interests.

Everyone has the right to rest and leisure, including reasonable limitation of working hours and periodic holidays with pay.

Everyone has the right to a standard of living adequate for the health and well-being of himself and of his family, including food, clothing, housing and medical care and necessary social services, and the right to security in the event of unemployment, sickness, disability, widowhood, old age or other lack of livelihood in circumstances beyond his control.

Motherhood and childhood are entitled to special care and assistance. All children, whether born in or out of wedlock, shall enjoy the same social protection.

Everyone has the right to education. Education shall be free, at least in the elementary and fundamental stages. Elementary education shall be compulsory. Technical and professional education shall be made generally available and higher education shall be equally accessible to all on the basis of merit. . . .

Everyone has the right freely to participate in the cultural life of the community, to enjoy the arts and to share in scientific advancement and its benefits. . . .

Everyone has duties to the community in which alone the free and full development of his personality is possible. . . .

Nothing in this Declaration may be interpreted as implying for any State, group or person any right to engage in any activity or to perform any act aimed at the destruction of any of the rights and freedoms set forth herein.

— Reading No. 24 —

BENTHAM: THE PRINCIPLE OF UTILITY[22]

Jeremy Bentham (1748-1832), founder of the philosophic school of Utilitarianism, inspired what in his day was considered an advanced form of liberalism, called radicalism. He had famous disciples: among them, James Mill, John Stuart Mill, David Ricardo, and the civil service reformer, Edwin Chadwick. In the following excerpt Bentham explains the meaning of Utilitarianism.

Nature has placed mankind under the governance of two sovereign masters, *pain* and *pleasure*. It is for them alone to point out what we ought to do, as well as to determine what we shall do. On the one hand the standard of right and wrong, on the other the chain of causes and effects, are fastened to their throne. They govern us in all we do, in all we say, in all we think: every effort we can make to throw off our subjection, will serve but to demonstrate and confirm it. . . . The *principle of utility* recognizes the subjection, and assumes it for the foundation of that system, the object of which is the rearing of the fabric of felicity by the hands of reason and of law. Systems which attempt to question it deal in sounds instead of sense, in caprice instead of reason, in darkness instead of light.

[22] Jeremy Bentham, *An Introduction to the Principles of Morals and Legislation* (Oxford, 1879), pp. 1-2.

— Reading No. 25 —

COBDEN: FREE TRADE AND UNIVERSAL PEACE[23]

Richard Cobden (1804-1865), English reformer and publicist, was a leading advocate of free trade. He was convinced that universal free trade would lead to world peace and prosperity. Cobden was highly influential in bringing about the repeal of the Corn Laws, in 1846, establishing Britain as a free trade country.

The following excerpt from a speech by Cobden explains his views concerning the advantages of free trade.

. . . I look farther; I see in the Free-trade principle that which shall act on the moral world as the principle of gravitation in the universe,—drawing men together, thrusting aside the antagonism of race, and creed, and language, and uniting us in the bonds of eternal peace. . . . I believe that the effect will be to change the face of the world, so as to introduce a system of government entirely distinct from that which now prevails. I believe that the desire and the motive for large and mighty empires; for gigantic armies and great navies . . . will die away; I believe that such things will cease to be necessary, or to be used when man becomes one family, and freely exchanges the fruits of his labour with his brother man. I believe that . . . the speculative philosopher of a thousand years hence will date the greatest revolution that ever happened in the world's history from the triumph of the principle which we have met here to advocate.

[23] Richard Cobden, *Speeches* (London, 1870), I, 362-363.

— Reading No. 26 —

MILL: NECESSITY OF WORKING CLASS REPRESENTATION[24]

John Stuart Mill (1806-1873) was the very incarnation of English liberalism. He exercised a profound influence on liberal thought, political, economic, and cultural, throughout the English-speaking world.

In the following excerpt Mill gives his view of what constitutes just representation.

✓ ✓ ✓

. . . We need not suppose that when power resides in an exclusive class, that class will knowingly and deliberately sacrifice the other classes to themselves: it suffices that, in the absence of its natural defenders, the interest of the excluded is always in danger of being overlooked; and, when looked at, is seen with very different eyes from those of the persons whom it directly concerns. In this country, for example, what are called the working classes may be considered as excluded from all direct participation in the government. . . . When a subject arises in which the labourers as such have an interest, is it regarded from any point of view but that of the employers of labour?

[24] John Stuart Mill, "Representative Government," *Utilitarianism, On Liberty, and Representative Government* (New York, 1914), p. 209.

— Reading No. 27 —

MILL: FREEDOM OF INDIVIDUAL OPINION[25]

To this day Mill's On Liberty *remains the classic exposition of freedom of opinion. This freedom, according to Mill, is to be protected not only against government censorship, but even more against the social tyranny of "prevailing opinion and feeling."*

The following excerpts give forceful illustrations of Mill's defense of intellectual liberty.

. . . The object of this Essay is to assert one very simple principle, as entitled to govern absolutely the dealings of society with the individual in the way of compulsion and control, whether the means used be physical force in the form of legal penalties, or the moral coercion of public opinion. That principle is, that the sole end for which mankind are warranted, individually or collectively, in interfering with the liberty of action of any of their number, is self-protection. That the only purpose for which power can be rightfully exercised over any member of a civilized community, against his will, is to prevent harm to others. His own good, either physical or moral, is not a sufficient warrant. . . . These are good reasons for remonstrating with him, or reasoning with him, or persuading him, or entreating him, but not for compelling him, or visiting him with any evil in case he do otherwise. To justify that, the conduct from which it is desired to deter him, must be calculated to produce

[25] John Stuart Mill, *Utilitarianism, On Liberty, and Representative Government* (New York, 1914), pp. 72-73, 68, 75, 79.

evil to some one else. The only part of the conduct of any one, for which he is amenable to society, is that which concerns others. In the part which merely concerns himself, his independence is, of right, absolute. Over himself, over his own body and mind, the individual is sovereign. . . .

. . . Society can and does execute its own mandates: and if it issues wrong mandates instead of right, or any mandates at all in things with which it ought not to meddle, it practises a social tyranny more formidable than many kinds of political oppression, since, though not usually upheld by such extreme penalties, it leaves fewer means of escape, penetrating more deeply into the details of life, and enslaving the soul itself. Protection, therefore, against the tyranny of the magistrate is not enough: there needs protection also against the tyranny of prevailing opinion and feeling, against the tendency of society to impose, by other means than civil penalties, its own ideas and practices as rules of conduct on those who dissent from them. . . .

But there is a sphere of action in which society, as distinguished from the individual, has, if any, only an indirect interest; comprehending all that portion of a person's life and conduct which affects only himself, or if it also affects others, only with their free, voluntary and undeceived consent and participation. . . . This then is the appropriate region of human liberty. It comprises, first, the inward domain of consciousness; demanding liberty of conscience in the most comprehensive sense; liberty of thought and feeling; absolute freedom of opinion and sentiment on all subjects, practical or speculative, scientific, moral, or theological. . . .

Let us suppose, therefore, that the government is entirely at one with the people, and never thinks of exerting any power of coercion unless in agreement with what it conceives to be their voice. But I deny the right of the people to exercise such coercion, either by themselves or by their government. The power itself is illegitimate. The best government has no more title to it than the worst. It is as noxious, or more noxious, when exerted in accordance with public opinion, than when in opposition to it. If all mankind minus one were of one opinion, and only one person were of the contrary opinion, mankind would be no more justified in silencing that one person, than he, if he had the power, would be justified in silencing mankind. Were an opinion a personal possession of no value except to the owner; if to be obstructed in the enjoyment of it were simply a private injury, it would make some difference whether the injury was inflicted only on a few persons or on many. But the peculiar evil of silencing the expression of an opinion is, that it is robbing the human race; posterity as well as the existing generation; those who dissent from the opinion, still more than those who hold it. If the opinion is right, they are deprived of the opportunity of exchanging error for truth: if wrong, they lose, what is almost as great a benefit, the cleaner perception and livelier impression of truth, produced by its collision with error. . . .

— Reading No. 28 —

THE PEOPLE'S CHARTER[26]

In Britain, shortly after the Reform Bill of 1832, a radical movement arose among the workers, who had been left unenfranchised. This movement, known as Chartism, demanded six political reforms. A petition, the People's Charter, was drawn up and presented to Parliament in 1848. It was rejected. However, since then, all the Points, except the one demanding annual Parliaments, have become law.

The following are the Six Points.

Equal Representation

That the United Kingdom be divided into 200 electoral districts; dividing, as nearly as possible, an equal number of inhabitants; and that each district do send a representative to Parliament.

Universal Suffrage

That every person producing proof of his being 21 years of age, to the clerk of the parish in which he has resided six months, shall be entitled to have his name registered as a voter. That the time for registering in each year be from the 1st of January to the 1st of March.

Annual Parliaments

That a general election do take place on the 24th of June in each year, and that each vacancy be filled up a

[26] William Lovett, *Life and Struggles of William Lovett* (New York, 1920), II, 456-457.

fortnight after it occurs. That the hours for voting be from six o'clock in the morning till six o'clock in the evening.

No Property Qualifications

That there shall be no property qualification for members; but on a requisition, signed by 200 voters, in favour of any candidate being presented to the clerk of the parish in which they reside, such candidate shall be put in nomination. And the list of all the candidates nominated throughout the district shall be stuck on the church door in every parish, to enable voters to judge of their qualification.

Vote by Ballot

That each voter must vote in the parish in which he resides. That each parish provide as many balloting boxes as there are candidates proposed in the district; and that a temporary place be fitted up in each parish church for the purpose of *secret voting*. And, on the day of election, as each voter passes orderly on to the ballot, he shall have given to him, by the officer in attendance, a balloting ball, which he shall drop into the box of his favourite candidate. At the close of the day the votes shall be counted, by the proper officers, and the numbers stuck on the church doors. The following day the clerk of the district and two examiners shall collect the votes of all the parishes throughout the district, and cause the name of the successful candidate to be posted in every parish of the district.

Sittings and Payments to Members

That the members do take their seats in Parliament on the first Monday in October next after their election, and continue their sittings every day (Sundays excepted) till the business of the sitting is terminated, but not later than the 1st of September. They shall meet every day (during the Session) for business at 10 o'clock in the morning, and adjourn at 4. And every member shall be paid quarterly out of the public treasury £400 a year. That all electoral officers shall be elected by universal suffrage.

— Reading No. 29 —

HOBHOUSE: STATE INTERVENTION[27]

Hobhouse was recognized as the leading British theorist of the newer liberalism, who renounced laissez faire in favor of state intervention.

In the following excerpt he proclaims his view of the state.

The central point of Liberal economics, then, is the equation of social service and reward. This is the principle that every function of social value requires such remuneration as serves to stimulate and maintain its effective performance; that every one who performs such a function has the right, in the strict ethical sense of that term, to such remuneration and to no more; that the residue of existing wealth should be at the disposal of the community for social purposes. . . . It is, indeed, implied that the State is vested with a certain overlordship over property in general and a supervisory power over industry in general, and this principle of economic sovereignty may be set side by side with that of economic justice as a no less fundamental conception of economic Liberalism.

[27] L. T. Hobhouse, *Liberalism* (London, 1911), pp. 209-210.

— Reading No. 30 —

AIMS OF THE BRITISH LABOR PARTY[28]

To secure for the producers by hand or by brain the full fruits of their industry, and the most equitable distribution thereof that may be possible, upon the basis of the common ownership of the means of production and the best obtainable system of popular administration and control of each industry and service; . . . acceptance, without reservations or qualifications, of the full implications of democracy, in their social, and economic, no less than in their political, significance.

[28] *Labour and the Nation* (London, 1928), issued by the British Labor Party.

— Reading No. 31 —

BEVERIDGE: SOCIAL SECURITY AS A DUTY OF THE STATE[29]

William Henry Beveridge (1879-), British economist and educator, became an outstanding advocate of social security. He concentrated on the problem of full employment as the basis of the Welfare State. In his Report on Social Insurance and Allied Services *(1942), Beveridge argued that mass unemployment was avoidable; and in his* Full Employment in a Free Society *(1945), he proposed detailed plans to create full employment through state action.*

The following excerpts indicate Beveridge's view of the necessity for social security.

✓ ✓ ✓

Full employment cannot be won and held without a great extension of the responsibilities and powers of the State exercized through organs of the central Government. No power less than that of the State can ensure adequate total outlay at all times, or can control, in the general interest, the location of industry and the use of land. . . . The proposals in this Report preserve absolutely all the essential liberties which are more precious than full employment itself. . . . Social Security today can be made the subject of a definite Plan and of legislation to give effect to that Plan. . . . Once a decision has been taken to abolish Want by comprehensive unified

[29] William H. Beveridge, *Full Employment in a Free Society* (New York, 1945), pp. 36, 38, 252, 254-255. Reprinted by permission of W. W. Norton and Company, Inc.

social insurance as the principal method, . . . the rest is administrative and actuarial detail. . . .

. . . If, on the other hand, the State is regarded as existing for the individual, a State which fails, in respect of many millions of individuals, to ensure them any opportunity of service and earning according to their powers or the possibility of a life free from the indignities and inquisitions of relief, is a State which has failed in a primary duty. . . .

The suggestion of this Report is that we should find a common objective in determination to make a Britain free of the giant evils of Want, Disease, Ignorance and Squalor. . . . We should regard Want, Disease, Ignorance and Squalor as common enemies of all of us, not as enemies with whom each individual may seek a separate peace, escaping himself to personal prosperity while leaving his fellows in their clutches. That is the meaning of social conscience; that one should refuse to make a separate peace with social evil. . . .

— Reading No. 32 —

GUIZOT: THE BOURGEOISIE, UPHOLDER OF FREEDOM[30]

François Guizot (1787-1874), statesman and historian, was the leading political figure in France during the reign of Louis Philippe, 1830-1848. Frankly and trenchantly he upheld the rule of the nation by the bourgeoisie on the ground that it gave a solid base to political freedom. As a bourgeois liberal, Guizot was bitterly opposed on the left by the democrats and socialists, and on the right by the reactionaries. When the regime of Louis Philippe was overthrown by the Revolution of 1848, Guizot was driven into exile.

The following excerpt is from a speech delivered by Guizot in the Chamber, on May 5, 1837.

✓ ✓ ✓

The middle classes, without privilege or limitation in the civil field and incessantly open in the political field to the upward movement of the entire nation, were, in our eyes, the best organs and the best guardians of the principles of 1789; of social order as of constitutional government, of liberty as of order, of civil liberties as of political liberty, of progress as of stability.

Following several general elections of which neither the freedom nor the legality could be seriously questioned, and exposed to incessantly repeated serious debates, the preponderant influence of the middle classes had brought about, in the Chambers and in the country, the formation

[30] *Source Book for History* 2. 1. Department of History, Brooklyn College, New York, 1949. Reprinted by permission of the Department of History, Brooklyn College.

of a majority which approved of the policy I have just explained, wished its maintenance and sustained it in the difficulties and trials, interior or exterior, which events imposed. This majority had been successively recruited, strengthened, trained for public life, and from day to day more intimately united to the government as the government was to it. According to the natural bent of representative and free government, it had become the (conservative) party which guarded the antirevolutionary and liberal policy, the success of which it had desired and assisted since 1831.

Parliamentary government, the practical form of a free government in a constitutional monarchy; the preponderant influence of the middle classes, efficacious guarantee of constitutional monarchy and of political liberties under this form of government; the conservative party, natural representative of the influence of the middle classes and necessary instrument of parliamentary government: these were, we were profoundly convinced, the means of action and the conditions for the continuance of the liberal and antirevolutionary policy, which we had it at heart to practice and maintain.

— Reading No. 33 —

GUIZOT: PROPERTY AND THE EXPANSION OF THE SUFFRAGE[31]

In this excerpt from the same speech, Guizot explains how the electorate, based on the bourgeoisie, will be expanded as a result of greater opportunities to acquire property.

✓ ✓ ✓

The electoral law has vested political power in the highest element of society, the element that is independent, enlightened, and capable. At the same time it has made provision for political power to expand downwards to the point where capacity ends. When, in the course of time, greater enlightenment and increase of wealth, those factors making for progress, have so changed the social order that a larger number of men and other classes have acquired capacity, the electorate will constantly be expanded. The very perfection of our system of government consists in the fact that political rights, limited by nature itself to those capable of exercizing them, are made subject to expansion as political capacity is acquired by more people. Furthermore, it possesses the great virtue of constantly encouraging the development of this capacity by spreading political enlightenment and knowledge of political matters. At the same time that it places a limit on political rights the system also endeavors to shift this limit, to extend it, to put it off, all with the object of elevating the entire nation.

[31] François Guizot, *Histoire parlementaire de France* (Paris, 1863), III, 104-105.

— Reading No. 34 —

TOCQUEVILLE: DEVELOPMENT OF THE PRINCIPLE OF EQUALITY[32]

In 1831 the Frenchman, Alexis de Tocqueville, at the age of 26, came to America. As a result of his voyage of intellectual discovery he wrote Democracy in America *(1835), a classic study of American democracy. What he beheld in America was a system of life and of government organized for the attainment of equality.*

The following excerpt gives Tocqueville's view of the human striving for equality.

✓ ✓ ✓

The various occurrences of national existence have everywhere turned to the advantage of democracy; all men have aided it by their exertions; those who have intentionally labored in its cause, and those who have served it unwittingly; those who have fought for it and those who have declared themselves its opponents, have all been driven along in the same track, have all labored to one end, some ignorantly and some unwillingly; all have been blind instruments in the hands of God.

The gradual development of the equality of conditions is, therefore, a providential fact, and it possesses all the characteristics of a Divine decree: it is universal, it is durable, it constantly eludes all human interference, and all events as well as all men contribute to its progress.

[32] Alexis de Tocqueville, *Democracy in America,* trans. Henry Reeve (New York, 1946), pp. 6-7.

Would it, then, be wise to imagine that a social impulse which dates from so far back can be checked by the efforts of a generation? Is it credible that the democracy which has annihilated the feudal system and vanquished kings will respect the citizen and the capitalists? Will it stop now that it has grown so strong and its adversaries so weak? None can say which way we are going, for all terms of comparison are wanting: the equality of conditions is more complete in Christian countries of the present day than it has been at any time or in any part of the world; so that the extent of what already exists prevents us from foreseeing what may be yet to come.

— Reading No. 35 —

GAMBETTA: DEMOCRACY AND FREEDOM[33]

Léon Gambetta (1838-1882), French statesman and orator, was the founder of the Third French Republic. In 1869, in opposition to the Second Empire, he ran as a candidate for the Chamber. During the campaign he delivered an address in which he proclaimed his belief in democracy. This address, known as the Belleville Manifesto, expounded the fundamental principles of the Radical party that dominated the policies of the Republic.

The following is an excerpt from the Belleville Manifesto.

With you, I think that there is no other sovereign but the people, and that universal suffrage, the instrument of this sovereignty, has no value and basis and carries no obligation, unless it be radically free. The most urgent reform must therefore be to free universal suffrage from every tutelage, every shackle, every pressure, every corruption. With you, I think that universal suffrage, once made the master, would suffice to sweep away all the things which your program demands, and to establish all the freedoms, all the institutions which we are seeking to bring about. With you, I think that France, the home of indestructible democracy, will know liberty, peace, order, justice, material prosperity, and moral greatness only

[33] Thomas C. Mendenhall and Others (eds.), *The Quest for a Principle of Authority in Europe, 1715-Present* (New York, 1948), p. 360. Reprinted by permission of Henry Holt and Company, Inc.

through the triumph of the principles of the French Revolution. With you, I think that a legal and loyal democracy is the political system par excellence which achieves most promptly and certainly the moral and material emancipation of the greatest number, and best ensures social equality in laws, actions, and customs.

But—with you also—I consider that the progressive achievement of these reforms depends absolutely on the political regime and on political reforms, and it is for me axiomatic in these matters that the form involves and determines the substance. It is, furthermore, this sequence and order of priority which our fathers have indicated and fixed in the profound and comprehensive slogan beyond which there is no safety: liberty, equality, fraternity. We are thus in mutual agreement. Our contract is completed. I am at once your delegate and your trustee. I go further than signifying agreement. I give you my vow: I swear obedience to this present contract and fidelity to the sovereign people.

— Reading No. 36 —

THE SAINT-MANDÉ PROGRAM[34]

A convention representing the various Socialist groups in France was held in Paris in 1896. A speech delivered by the Socialist leader, Alexandre Millerand, was approved by the convention, and became the charter of French socialism, known as the "Saint-Mandé Program."

The following excerpt from Millerand's speech abjures revolution, and favors democratic methods to attain socialism.

✓ ✓ ✓

Socialism does aim at securing for every human being, by a beneficent and quite natural transformation, these two twin blessings, liberty and property, of which the capitalistic *régime* inevitably robs him. But in thus indicating the end which our party pursues, I have answered beforehand the ridiculous charge, so often made, that it expects its ideas to triumph only by violent revolution. Our eminent friend, Gabriel Deville, whom the Fourth Constituency will send next Sunday to sit with us in the Socialist group at the Chamber, said some days ago, strongly and definitely, that we could get the social transformation from no rebel minority, but from a majority with a purpose. Resort to force?—for whom and against whom? Republicans before everything, we do not indulge the crazy idea of appealing to a pretender's sham prestige or a dictator's sword to secure the triumph of our doctrines. We appeal only to universal suffrage. It is the voter whom we want to set economically and politically free. We

[34] R. C. K. Ensor (ed.), *Modern Socialism* (New York, 1904), pp. 53-54.

claim only the right of persuading him. . . . To realize the immediate reforms capable of relieving the lot of the working class, and thus fitting it to win its own freedom, and to begin, as conditioned by the nature of things, the socialization of the means of production, it is necessary and sufficient for the Socialist party to endeavor to capture the Government through universal suffrage. . . .

Such, citizens, are in my opinion the three essential points which are necessary to characterize a Socialistic programme—intervention of the State to convert from capitalistic into national property the different categories of the means of production and exchange in proportion as they become ripe for social appropriation; capture of Government through universal suffrage; international understanding between the workers.

— Reading No. 37 —

MAZZINI: NATIONALISM AND DEMOCRACY[35]

Joseph Mazzini (1805-1872), Italian nationalist and democrat, was both a philosopher and a man of action. He was indefatigable in promoting the cause of Italian unity, on the basis of a democratic Republic. Mazzini was inspired by an almost religious view of nationalism as a great advance of mankind. Let it be understood that his nationalism was completely liberal. In founding "Young Italy" and "Young Europe" Mazzini stressed liberty, equality, and humanity as well as independence and unity.

The following excerpts express Mazzini's philosophy of nationalism.

✓ ✓ ✓

. . . A Country is not a mere territory; the particular territory is only its foundation. The Country is the idea which rises upon that foundation; it is the sentiment of love, the sense of fellowship which binds together all the sons of that territory. So long as a single one of your brothers is not represented by his own vote in the development of the national life—so long as a single one vegetates uneducated among educated—so long as a single one able and willing to work languishes in poverty for want of work—you have not got a Country such as it ought to be, the Country of all and for all. *Votes, education, work* are the three main pillars of the nation; do not rest until your hands have solidly erected them.

[35] Joseph Mazzini, *The Duties of Man and Other Essays* (New York, 1915), p. 58; *Life and Writings* (London, 1864-1866), I, 96-112; *ibid.* III, 33-34.

Young Italy is *Republican and Unitarian.*

Republican—because theoretically every nation is destined, by the law of God and humanity, to form a free and equal community of brothers; and the republican is the only form of government that insures this future.

Because all true sovereignty resides essentially in the nation, the sole and progressive and continuous interpreter of the supreme moral law. . . .

Young Italy is *Unitarian*—

Because, without unity, there is no true nation.

Because, without unity there is no real strength; and Italy, surrounded as she is by powerful, united, and jealous nations, has need of strength before all things. . . .

National unity, as understood by Young Italy, does not imply the despotism of any, but the association and concord of all. The life inherent in each locality is sacred. Young Italy would have the *administrative* organization designed upon a broad basis of religious respect for the liberty of each commune, but the political organization, destined to represent the nation in Europe, should be one and central. . . .

Every people has its special mission, which will cooperate towards the fulfilment of the general mission of humanity. That mission constitutes its *nationality*. Nationality is sacred. . . .

Humanity will only be truly constituted when all the peoples of which it is composed have acquired the free exercise of their sovereignty, and shall be associated in a Republican Confederation, governed and directed by a common Declaration of Principles and a common Past, towards the common aim—the discovery and fulfilment of the Universal Moral Law. . . .

— Reading No. 38 —

HEGEL: THE STATE AS THE DIVINE IDEA[36]

Georg W. F. Hegel (1770-1831) had a profound influence on German political philosophy. The state, in his view, was the decisive factor in history. In it was comprehended all morality and all power, hence whatever it did was right. The worship of the state, so marked in Germany, was largely of Hegelian inspiration.

The following excerpt explains the nature of the state according to Hegel.

✓ ✓ ✓

In the history of the World, only those peoples can come under our notice which form a state. For it must be understood that this latter is the realization of Freedom, i.e. of the absolute final aim, and that it exists for its own sake. It must further be understood that all the worth which the human being possesses—all spiritual reality, he possesses only through the State. For his spiritual reality consists in this, that his own essence—Reason—is objectively present to him, that it possesses objective immediate existence for him. Thus only is he fully conscious; thus only is he a partaker of morality—of a just and moral social and political life. For Truth is the Unity of the universal and subjective Will; and the Universal is to be found in the State, in its laws, its universal and rational arrangements. The State is the Divine Idea as it exists on Earth. We have in it, therefore, the object of History in a more definite shape than before; that in which Freedom

[36] G. W. F. Hegel, *Lectures on the Philosophy of History*, trans. J. Sibree (New York, 1899), p. 39.

obtains objectivity, and lives in the enjoyment of this objectivity. For Law is the objectivity of Spirit; volition in its true form. Only that will which obeys law, is free; for it obeys itself—it is independent and so free. When the State or our country constitutes a community of existence; when the subjective will of man submits to laws—the contradiction between Liberty and Necessity vanishes. The Rational has necessary existence, as being the reality and substance of things, and we are free in recognizing it as law, and following it as the substance of our own being. The objective and the subjective will are then reconciled, and present one identical homogeneous whole. For the morality (*Sitt-lichkeit*) of the State is not of that ethical (*moralische*) reflective kind, in which one's own conviction bears sway; this latter is rather the peculiarity of the modern time, while the true antique morality is based on the principle of abiding by one's duty (to the state at large).

— Reading No. 39 —

THE FUNDAMENTAL RIGHTS OF THE GERMAN PEOPLE[37]

This declaration of human rights, adopted by the Frankfort Assembly in 1848, was later suppressed.

The following excerpts are from the most important articles.

✓ ✓ ✓

The following fundamental rights shall be guaranteed to the German people. They shall serve as a standard for the constitutions of the separate German states, and no constitution or legislation of any German state may ever set aside or limit them.

The German people consists of the citizens of the states which make up the German Reich. Every German has the rights of German citizenship. He may exercise these rights in every German state. The election laws of the Reich determine the right to vote in elections for the Reich's assembly. Every German has the right to sojourn or establish his residence in any part of the territory of the Reich, to acquire real estate of any description and to control the same, to engage in any trade, to enjoy the rights of local citizenship. The government of the Reich shall establish for the whole of Germany the conditions governing sojourn and residence by a law of residence and those respecting trades by trade regulations. No German state may make a distinction in matters of civil and

[37] Columbia University, *Introduction to Contemporary Civilization in the West* (New York, 1946). Reprinted by permission of Columbia University Press and the Contemporary Civilization Staff of Columbia College.

criminal law and procedural rights between its citizens and other Germans which would place the latter in the category of aliens. . . .

No privilege of rank is valid before the law. Nobility is abolished as a rank. All privileges of rank are abolished. All Germans are equal before the law. All titles, in so far as they do not pertain to an office, are abolished. . . .

The freedom of the individual is inviolable. The arrest of a person shall take place, except in case of his being apprehended in the deed, only on the authority of a court order stating the cause. . . . The home is inviolable. The searching of a domicile is permissible only: (1) on authority of a judicial order stating reasons, which order must be presented to the parties concerned immediately or within the following twenty-four hours; (2) in case of pursuit of an offender caught in the act on the part of legally authorized officials. . . .

Every German has the right to express his opinion freely in speaking, writing, printing, or pictorial representation. . . .

Every German has full freedom of belief and of conscience. No one is obligated to reveal his religious convictions. Every German is unrestricted in the common practice of his religion at home or in public. . . .

Science and the teaching of science are free. Instruction and the system of education are under the supervision of the state and are, with the exception of religious instruction, freed from the supervision of the clergy as such. Every German is free to establish, to lead, and to give instruction in institutions for instruction and education, if he has given evidence of his qualifications to do so to the proper authorities of the state. . . . Sufficient provision shall everywhere be made for the education of German youth through public schools. . . .

Every German has the right to apply in writing to the authorities, to the representatives, and to the Reichstag with requests and complaints. . . .

Germans have the right to assemble peacefully and without arms; no special permission to do so is required. . . .

Private property is inviolable. Expropriation may take place only in the interest of the public welfare, only according to law and on the basis of just compensation.

Ecclesiastical property shall be protected by legislation. . . . Every relationship of bondage or serfdom is ended forever. The following are abolished without compensation: (1) the patrimonial jurisdiction and the police power of the lord of the manor, together with the authority, exemptions, and imposts emanating therefrom; (2) the personal imposts and services which have their source in the manorial and feudal relationship. . . . The right to hunt on the property of others, hunting services and fees, or other services for purposes of hunting are abolished without compensation. . . . All feudal relations are to be annulled. . . . Taxation shall be so regulated that the privileged position of some occupations and property shall cease in the community and the state.

Every German state shall have a constitution with representation of the people. Ministers are responsible to the representatives of the people. The representatives of the people have a decisive voice in legislation, in taxation, in the regulation of affairs of state. Also, in case there is a bicameral legislature, each chamber has for itself the right of initiating legislation, presenting grievances, of petitioning, as well as of impeaching ministers. The sessions of the representatives are as a rule public.

The non-German speaking races of Germany are guaranteed their racial development, namely the equal right of their languages in the regions which they occupy, their rights in church affairs, in instruction, in local government, and in administration of justice. . . .

— Reading No. 40 —

TROELTSCH: THE GERMAN VIEW OF FREEDOM[38]

Ernst Troeltsch (1865-1923), German social and religious philosopher, had a deep understanding of the nature of German liberalism. His book, The German Idea of Freedom *(1916), explains the historical and cultural bases of German liberalism, so different from that of other Western nations.*

The following excerpt explains the German view of liberty in relation to duty.

✓ ✓ ✓

Liberty as creative participation in the formation of state authority means to us, not the bringing forth of governmental will out of individual wills, not control of the mandatory by the principal, but the free, conscious and dutiful dedication of oneself to the whole, as it has been molded by history, state and nation. The whole as the expression and incarnation of collectivity is to be willed freely and always re-create anew in personal activity. Thus, prince and officials consider themselves as the first servants of the state, and citizens think of themselves as members of the state. They are all organs of the one sovereign whole which they bring forth anew in ceaseless self-devotion. Liberty consists more in duties than in rights, or, rather, in rights which are simultaneously duties. The individuals do not compose the whole, but identify themselves with it. Liberty is not equality, but

[38] William Ebenstein (ed.), *Modern Political Thought: The Great Issues* (New York, 1947), pp. 256-257. Reprinted by permission of Rinehart and Company, Inc.

service of the individual in his station organically due to him. In this, lie the dignity and active participation of the individual, but also his restraint, and all modern achievements of national unity, equality before the law, parliaments and universal military service, are molded by this spirit. This is the "state mysticism" (*Staatsmystik*) which our great thinkers and historians have felt in common with Plato. . . . This spirit has created all that is great in the past German century, it characterizes two expressions of life so contrary to one another as the German army and the socialist party. It has also absorbed, and digested, Bismarck's realism.

— Reading No. 41 —

TREITSCHKE: THE STATE AS POWER[39]

Heinrich von Treitschke (1834-1896), German historian and political scientist, was a truculent upholder of the theory of Machtpolitik, *according to which, power constituted the very essence of the state. He strongly opposed such liberal ideas as natural rights and self-government.*

The following excerpt gives Treitschke's view of the state.

On close examination then, it becomes clear that if the State is power, only that State which has power realizes its own idea, and this accounts for the undeniably ridicu-

[39] Heinrich von Treitschke, *Politics,* trans. B. Dugdale and T. de Bille (New York, 1916), I, 34-35. Reprinted by permission of Macmillan Company.

lous element which we discern in the existence of a small State. Weakness is not itself ridiculous, except when masquerading as strength. In small States that puling spirit is hatched, which judges the State by the taxes it levies, and does not perceive that if the State may not enclose and repress like an egg-shell, neither can it protect. Such thinkers fail to understand that the moral benefits for which we are indebted to the State are above all price. It is by generating this form of materialism that small States have so deleterious an effect upon their citizens.

Moreover, they are totally lacking in that capacity for justice which characterizes their greater neighbors. Any person who has plenty of relations and is not a perfect fool is soon provided for in a small country, while in a large one, although justice tends to become stereotyped, it is not possible to be so much influenced by personal and local circumstances as in the narrower sphere. . . .

Everything considered, therefore, we reach the conclusion that the large State is the nobler type. This is more especially true of its fundamental functions such as wielding the sword in defence of the hearth and of justice. Both are better protected by a large State than a small one. The latter cannot wage war with any prospect of success. . . .

— Reading No. 42 —

BISMARCK: STATE INTERVENTION TO PROTECT THE WORKERS[40]

Bismarck created a sensation when, as Chancellor of the German Empire, he sponsored compulsory social insurance for the workers. He strongly opposed the policy of laissez faire, advocated by the bourgeois liberals, because he believed that a paternalistic government would allay discontent among the workers by laws giving them a degree of economic security. The following excerpt is from a speech by Bismarck in the Reichstag.

Deputy Richter has called attention to the responsibility of the state for what it does, in the area now concerned. Well, gentlemen, I have a feeling that the state may also be responsible for its omissions. I am not of the opinion that "*laisser faire, laisser aller,*" "pure Manchesterism in politics," "as you make your bed, so you must lie," "every man for himself, and Devil take the hindmost," "to him that hath shall be given, and from him that hath not shall be taken away even that which he hath," have applicability in a state, especially a monarchical, paternalistic state; on the contrary, I believe that those who thus condemn the intervention of the state for the protection of the weaker are themselves suspect of wishing to exploit the strength they have, be it capitalistic, be it rhetorical, be it what it may, to gain a following, to oppress others, to build party dominance, and of becoming annoyed as soon as this understanding is disturbed by any influence of the government.

[40] Source Book for History 2. 1, Vol II. Department of History, Brooklyn College, 1949: (Otto von Bismarck, *Die gesammelten Werke,* Berlin, 1929, XII, 236-249.)

— Reading No. 43 —

THE NORTHWEST ORDINANCE OF 1787[41]

Even before the adoption of the Constitution, Congress, under the Articles of Confederation, registered one of its greatest achievements by adopting, on July 13, 1787, the Northwest Ordinance. It was later accepted by the government under the Constitution.

The following excerpts give the most important provisions of the Ordinance.

✓ ✓ ✓

And for extending the fundamental principles of civil and religious liberty, which form the basis whereon these republics, their laws and constitutions are erected; to fix and establish those principles as the basis of all laws, constitutions, and governments, which forever hereafter shall be formed in the said territory; to provide also for the establishment of states, and permanent government therein, and for their admission to a share in the federal councils on an equal footing with the original states, at as early periods as may be consistent with the general interest:

It is hereby ordained and declared by the authority aforesaid, That the following articles shall be considered as articles of compact, between the original states and the people and states in the said territory, and forever remain unalterable, unless by common consent, to wit:

ARTICLE 1. No person, demeaning himself in a peaceable and orderly manner, shall ever be molested on

[41] T. C. Pease and A. S. Roberts (eds.), *Selected Readings in American History* (New York, 1928), pp. 171-176.

account of his mode of worship or religious sentiments in the said territory.

ARTICLE 2. The inhabitants of the said territory shall always be entitled to the benefits of the writ of habeas corpus and of the trial by jury; of a proportionate representation of the people in the legislature; and of judicial proceedings according to the course of the common law. All persons shall be bailable, unless for capital offenses, where the proof shall be evident, or the presumption great. All fines shall be moderate; and no cruel or unusual punishments shall be inflicted. No man shall be deprived of his liberty or property, but by the judgment of his peers or the law of the land; and should the public exigencies make it necessary, for the common preservation, to take any person's property, or to demand his particular services, full compensation shall be made for the same. And, in the just preservation of rights and property, it is understood and declared, that no law ought ever to be made or have force in the said territory, that shall, in any manner whatever, interfere with or affect private contracts or engagements, bona fide, and without fraud previously formed. . . .

ARTICLE 6. There shall be neither slavery nor involuntary servitude in the said territory, otherwise than in punishment of crimes whereof the party shall have been duly convicted: *Provided, always,* that any person escaping into the same, from whom labor or service is lawfully claimed in any one of the original states, such fugitive may be lawfully reclaimed, and conveyed to the person claiming his or her labor or services as aforesaid.

— Reading No. 44 —

JEFFERSON: TOLERATION OF POLITICAL DIFFERENCES[42]

Thomas Jefferson's accession to the Presidency, was regarded as a sort of revolution. As the protagonist of democratic liberalism he inspired distrust, even fear, among his conservative opponents. Throughout his public life his activities were dedicated to the advancement of popular rule.

The following excerpt from his First Inaugural Address states his principles firmly but in a spirit of moderation.

During the contest of opinion through which we have passed, the animation of discussions and of exertions has sometimes worn an aspect which might impose on strangers unused to think freely and to speak and to write what they think; but this being now decided by the voice of the nation, announced according to the rules of the Constitution, all will, of course, arrange themselves under the will of the law, and unite in common efforts for the common good. All, too, will bear in mind this sacred principle, that though the will of the majority is in all cases to prevail, that will to be rightful must be reasonable; that the minority possess their equal rights, which equal law must protect, and to violate would be oppression. . . .

But every difference of opinion is not a difference of principle. We have called by different names brethren of the same principle. We are all Republicans, we are all Federalists. If there be any among us who would wish to

[42] T. C. Pease and A. S. Roberts (eds.), *Selected Readings in American History* (New York, 1928), p. 232.

dissolve this Union or to change its republican form, let them stand undisturbed as monuments of the safety with which error of opinion may be tolerated where reason is left free to combat it. I know, indeed, that some honest men fear that a republican government cannot be strong, that this government is not strong enough; but would the honest patriot, in the full tide of successful experiment, abandon a government which has so far kept us free and firm on the theoretic and visionary fear that this government, the world's best hope, may by possibility want energy to preserve itself? I trust not. I believe this, on the contrary, the strongest government on earth. I believe it the only one where every man, at the call of the law, would fly to the standard of the law, and would meet invasions of the public order as his own personal concern. Sometimes it is said that man cannot be trusted with the government of himself. Can he, then, be trusted with the government of others? Or have we found angels in the forms of kings to govern him? Let history answer this question.

— Reading No. 45 —

LINCOLN: THE MEANING OF EQUALITY[43]

In an address delivered on June 26, 1857, Lincoln discussed the implication of the Dred Scott decision of the Supreme Court. According to this famous decision, Congress could not prohibit slavery in the Territories,

[43] William Ebenstein (ed.), *Modern Political Thought: The Great Issues* (New York, 1947), p. 86. Reprinted by permission of Rinehart & Co., Inc.

and Negroes could not sue in the federal courts. The following excerpt is from Lincoln's address.

✓ ✓ ✓

I think the authors of that notable instrument [the Declaration of Independence] intended to include *all* men, but they did not intend to declare all men equal *in all respects*. They did not mean to say all were equal in color, size, intellect, moral developments, or social capacity. They defined with tolerable distinctness in what respects they did consider all men created equal—equal with "certain unalienable rights, among which are life, liberty, and the pursuit of happiness." This they said, and this they meant. They did not mean to assert the obvious untruth that all men were then actually enjoying that equality, nor yet that they were about to confer it immediately upon them. In fact, they had no power to confer such a boon. They meant simply to declare the right, so that enforcement of it might follow as fast as circumstances should permit.

They meant to set up a standard maxim for free society, which should be familiar to all, and revered by all; constantly looked to, constantly labored for, and even though never perfectly attained, constantly approximated, and thereby constantly spreading and deepening its influence and augmenting the happiness and value of life to all people of all colors everywhere. The assertion that "all men are created equal" was of no practical use in effecting our separation from Great Britain; and it was placed in the Declaration not for that, but for future use. Its authors meant it to be—as, thank God, it is now proving itself—a stumbling block to all those who in after times might seek to turn a free people back into the hateful paths of despotism. They knew the proneness of prosperity to breed tyrants, and they meant when such should appear in this fair land and commence their vocation, they should find left for them at least one hard nut to crack.

— Reading No. 46 —

LINCOLN: THE GETTYSBURG ADDRESS

After the Union victory of the Battle of Gettysburg, Lincoln delivered this memorable address on November 9, 1863. It is brief, beautifully phrased, and truly Lincolnian in its sentiments.

Fourscore and seven years ago our fathers brought forth on this continent, a new nation, conceived in liberty, and dedicated to the proposition that all men are created equal.

Now we are engaged in a great civil war, testing whether that nation, or any nation so conceived and so dedicated, can long endure. We are met on a great battle-field of that war. We have come to dedicate a portion of that field, as a final resting-place for those who here gave their lives that that nation might live. It is altogether fitting and proper that we should do this.

But, in a larger sense, we cannot dedicate—we cannot consecrate—we cannot hallow—this ground. The brave men, living and dead, who struggled here, have consecrated it, far above our poor power to add or detract. The world will little note, nor long remember what we say here, but it can never forget what they did here. It is for us the living, rather, to be dedicated here to the unfinished work which they who fought here have thus far so nobly advanced. It is rather for us to be here dedicated to the great task remaining before us—that from these honored dead we take increased devotion to that cause for which they gave the last full measure of devotion—that we here highly resolve that these dead shall not have died in vain—that this nation, under God, shall have a new birth of freedom—and that government of the people, by the people, for the people, shall not perish from the earth.

— Reading No. 47 —

THE CIVIL WAR AMENDMENTS TO THE CONSTITUTION

These Amendments were adopted as a result of the victory of the North over the South; the Thirteenth, on December 18, 1865; the Fourteenth, on July 28, 1868; and the Fifteenth, on March 30, 1870.

Thirteenth Amendment

Section 1. Neither slavery nor involuntary servitude, except as a punishment for crime whereof the party shall have been duly convicted, shall exist within the United States, or any place subject to their jurisdiction.

Section 2. Congress shall have power to enforce this article by appropriate legislation.

Fourteenth Amendment

Section 1. All persons born or naturalized in the United States, and subject to the jurisdiction thereof, are citizens of the United States and of the State wherein they reside. No State shall make or enforce any law which shall abridge the privileges or immunities of citizens of the United States; nor shall any State, deprive any person of life, liberty, or property, without due process of law, nor deny to any person within its jurisdiction the equal protection of the laws.

Section 2. Representatives shall be apportioned among the several States according to their respective numbers, counting the whole number of persons in each State, excluding Indians not taxed. But when the right to vote at any election . . . is denied to any of the male inhabitants of such State, . . . the basis of representation therein shall be reduced in the proportion which the number of such male citizens shall bear to the whole number of male citizens twenty-one years of age in such State. . . .

The Fifteenth Amendment

Section 1. The right of citizens of the United States to vote shall not be denied or abridged by the United States or by any State on account of race, color, or previous condition of servitude.

Section 2. The Congress shall have power to enforce this article by appropriate legislation.

— Reading No. 48 —

BRANDEIS: POLITICAL LIBERTY AND INDUSTRIAL ABSOLUTISM[44]

Louis D. Brandeis (1856-1941) was an American lawyer who served as an Associate Justice of the Supreme Court, 1916-1939. He combined great technical ability as a jurist with a generous vision of the new American liberalism. Brandeis' judicial opinions became noted for their favorable attitude toward government intervention in economic matters.

[44] William Ebenstein (ed.), *Modern Political Thought: The Great Issues* (New York, 1947), pp. 506-507. Reprinted by permission of Rinehart and Co., Inc.

The following excerpt is taken from his testimony before the Commission on Industrial Relations, January 23, 1915.

My observation leads me to believe that while there are many contributing causes to [industrial] unrest, that there is one cause which is fundamental. That is the necessary conflict—the contrast between our political liberty and our industrial absolutism. We are as free politically, perhaps, as free as it is possible for us to be. Every male has his voice and vote; and the law has endeavored to enable, and has succeeded practically, in enabling him to exercise his political franchise without fear. He therefore has his part; and certainly can secure an adequate part in the government of the country in all of its political relations; that is, in all relations which are determined directly by legislation or governmental administration.

On the other hand, in dealing with industrial problems the position of the ordinary worker is exactly the reverse. The individual employee has no effective voice or vote. And the main objection, as I see it, to the very large corporation is, that it makes possible—and in many cases makes inevitable—the exercise of industrial absolutism. It is not merely the case of the individual worker against the employer which, even if he is a reasonably sized employer, presents a serious situation calling for the interposition of a union to protect the individual. But we have the situation of an employer so potent, so well organized, with such concentrated forces and with such extraordinary powers of reserve and the ability to endure against strikes and other efforts of a union, that the relatively loosely organized masses of even strong unions are unable to cope with the situation. We are dealing here with a question, not of motive, but of condition. Now, the large corporation and the managers of the powerful corporation are probably in large part actuated by motives just the same as an employer of a tenth of their size. Neither of them, as a rule, wishes to have his liberty abridged; but the smaller concern usually comes to the conclusion that it is necessary that it should be, where an important union must be dealt with. But when a great financial power has developed—when there exists these powerful organizations, which can successfully summon forces from all parts of the country, which can afford to use tremendous amounts of money in any conflict to carry out what they deem to be their business principle, and can also afford to suffer large losses—you have necessarily a condition of inequality between the two contending forces. Such contests, though undertaken with the best motives and with strong conviction on the part of the corporate managers that they are seeking what is for the best interests not only of the company but of the community, lead to absolutism. The result, in the cases of these large corporations, may be to develop a benevolent absolutism, but it is an absolutism all the same; and it is that which makes the great corporation so dangerous. There develops within the State a state so powerful that the ordinary social and industrial forces existing are insufficient to cope with it.

— Reading No. 49 —

FRANKLIN D. ROOSEVELT: A NEW BILL OF RIGHTS[45]

In his message to the Congress (January 11, 1944), President Franklin D. Roosevelt asserted his belief in the fundamental principles of what is now called the "Welfare State." In the following excerpt from the message he proclaimed "a second Bill of Rights."

✓ ✓ ✓

We have come to a clear realization of the fact that true individual freedom cannot exist without economic security and independence. "Necessitous men are not free men." People who are hungry and out of a job are the stuff of which dictatorships are made.

[45] F. D. Roosevelt, *Nothing to Fear* (Boston, 1946), p. 396.

In our day these economic truths have become accepted as self-evident. We have accepted, so to speak, a second Bill of Rights under which a new basis of security and prosperity can be established for all—regardless of station, race or creed.

Among these are:

The right to a useful and remunerative job in the industries or shops or farms or mines of the nation;

The right to earn enough to provide adequate food and clothing and recreation;

The right of every farmer to raise and sell his products at a return which will give him and his family a decent living;

The right of every business man, large and small, to trade in an atmosphere of freedom from unfair competition and domination by monopolies at home or abroad;

The right of every family to a decent home;

The right to adequate protection from the economic fears of old age, sickness, accident and unemployment;

The right to a good education.

All of these rights spell security. . . . For unless there is security here at home there cannot be lasting peace in the world.

— Reading No. 50 —

DECISION OF THE SUPREME COURT AGAINST SEGREGATION IN PUBLIC SCHOOLS[46]

On May 17, 1954, a unanimous decision of the Supreme Court, in the case of Brown *v.* Board of Education of

[46] From a pamphlet issued by the National Association for the Advancement of Colored People.

Topeka (347 U.S. 483) *declared unconstitutional laws of state and local governments establishing segregation of Negroes in the public schools.*

The following are excerpts from this decision.

✓ ✓ ✓

Today, education is perhaps the most important function of state and local governments. Compulsory school attendance laws and the great expenditures for education both demonstrate our recognition of the importance of education to our democratic society. It is required in the performance of our most basic public responsibilities, even service in the armed forces. It is the very foundation of good citizenship. Today it is a principal instrument in awakening the child to cultural values, in preparing him for later professional training, and in helping him to adjust normally to his environment. In these days, it is doubtful that any child may reasonably be expected to succeed in life if he is denied the opportunity of an education. Such an opportunity, where the state has undertaken to provide it, is a right which must be made available to all on equal terms.

We come then to the question presented: Does segregation of children in public schools solely on the basis of race, even though the physical facilities and other "tangible" factors may be equal, deprive the children of the minority group of equal educational opportunities? We believe that it does. . . . Such considerations apply with added force to children in grade and high schools. To separate them from others of similar age and qualifications solely because of their race generates a feeling of inferiority as to their status in the community that may affect their hearts and minds in a way unlikely ever to be undone. . . .

We conclude that in the field of public education the doctrine of "separate but equal" has no place. Separate educational facilities are inherently unequal. Therefore, we hold that the plaintiffs and others similarly situated for whom the actions have been brought are, by reason on the segregation complained of, deprived of the equal protection of the laws guaranteed by the Fourteenth Amendment. . . .

A SELECT BIBLIOGRAPHY

Blease, W. L., *A Short History of English Liberalism* (New York, 1913).

Bullock, A. and Shock, M. (eds.), *The Liberal Tradition. From Fox to Keynes* (New York, 1956).

Clokie, H. McD., *The Origin and Nature of Constitutional Government* (London, 1936).

Croce, Benedetto, *History of Europe in the Nineteenth Century,* tr. by Henry Furst (New York, 1933).

Curti, Merle, *The Growth of American Thought* (New York, 1943).

Dewey, John, *Liberalism and Social Action* (New York, 1935).

Ekirch, Arthurs A., Jr., *The Decline of American Liberalism* (New York, 1955).

Hallowell, J. H., *The Decline of Liberalism as an Ideology* (Berkeley and Los Angeles, 1943).

Hartz, Louis, *The Liberal Tradition in America* (New York, 1955).

Havens, George R., *The Age of Ideas* (New York, 1955).

Hobhouse, Leonard T., *Liberalism* (London, 1911).

Hobson, John A., *The Crisis of Liberalism* (London, 1909).

Hofstadter, Richard, *The Age of Reform* (New York, 1955).

Kohn, Hans, *American Nationalism* (New York, 1957).

Laski, Harold J., *The Rise of European Liberalism* (London, 1936).

Lauterpacht, Hersh, *An International Bill of the Rights of Man* (New York, 1945).

Martin, Kingsley, *The Rise of French Liberal Thought* (New York, 1954).

Neill, T. P., *The Rise and Decline of Liberalism* (Milwaukee, 1953).

Pennock, J. R., *Liberal Democracy* (New York, 1950).

Ruggiero, Guido de, *The History of European Liberalism,* tr. by R. G. Collingwood (London, 1927).

Salvemini, Gaetano, *Mazzini,* tr. by I. M. Rawson (Stanford University Press, 1956).

Schapiro, J. Salwyn, *Condorcet and the Rise of Liberalism* (New York, 1934).

——— *Liberalism and the Challenge of Fascism* (New York, 1949).

Schlesinger, Arthur M., Jr., *The Vital Center* (Boston, 1949).

Snyder, Louis L., *German Nationalism: The Tragedy of a People* (Harrisburg, 1952).

Stearns, Harold (ed.), *Liberalism in America* (New York, 1919).

Watkins, Frederick, *The Political Traditions of the West. A Study in the Development of Modern Liberalism* (Cambridge, 1948).

INDEX

Abélard, Peter, 14, 96-97
Adenauer, Konrad, 77
Age of Reason, *see* Enlightenment
American Constitutional Convention, 78
American Revolution, 28-29
Anti-clericalism, 12, 29, 42, 56-57, 63, 64
Anti-imperialism, 44, 49, 59, 78, 88, 175
Asquith, Herbert H., 47
Attlee, Clement, 48

Bentham, Jeremy, 41
Beveridge, William, 37, 153-154
Bill of Rights, American, 29, 78, 85, 126-127, 184-185; English, 28, 40, 122-123; German, 70, 72, 75, 77; Italian, 66
Bismarck, Otto von, 71ff., 174
Blum, Léon, 58
Boulanger Affair, 55-56
Brandeis, Louis, 182-184
Bright, John, 41, 42
Bryan, William J., 83

Capitalism, 21-23, 27, 32-34, 52, 53, 62, 74, 79, 80, 83, 112-114, 183-184
Cavour, 62-63
Chartism, 46, 149-150
Classical Economy, 32-33
Cobden, Richard, 41, 42, 144
Commune, Paris, 55
Communism, 59, 65, 67, 76, 77, 88, 89
Condorcet, 18, 21, 103-104, 109-111
Constant, Benjamin, 51
Contract, social, 23, 25, 78, 120-121

Declaration of Independence, 11, 28, 124-125
Declaration of the Rights of Man, 9, 11, 128-130
Democracy, 25, 28-29, 36, 45-47, 53, 55, 58, 62, 70, 75, 77, 80, 115ff., 121, 149, 152, 160-164
Descartes, René, 15, 100
Dewey, John, 138
Diderot, Denis, 16, 20
Disraeli, Benjamin, 46
Dreyfus Affair, 56, 57

Education, 20-21, 36, 46, 57, 64, 67, 81, 87, 109-111, 142, 169, 185-186
Encyclopedia, French, 20
English Revolution of 1688, 27
Enlightenment, 16, 26, 77
Equality, 10, 28-30, 179, 181-182
Erasmus, Desiderius, 15, 98ff.

Fascism, 66, 76, 88
Frankfort Assembly, 70-71
Free trade, 23, 44, 132, 144
French Revolution, 21, 29-30, 50

Fundamental Rights of the German Nation, 70, 71, 168-170

Gambetta, Léon, 55, 160-161
George, David Lloyd, 47
German Federal Republic, 76
Gladstone, William E., 44, 46
Guizot, François, 52-53, 54, 153-157

Hamilton, Alexander, 80
Hegel, Georg Wilhelm, 69, 166-167
Hitler, Adolph, 76
Hobhouse, L. T., 10, 93, 151
Holmes, Oliver Wendell, 11

Individualism, 9, 45, 89, 93, 112-113, 118, 146-147, 169
Industrial Revolution, 31, 80

Jaurès, Jean, 58
Jefferson, Thomas, 16, 21, 80, 177-178
"June Days' of 1848, 55

Kant, Immanuel, 16, 19
Keynes, John M., 37

Laissez faire, 22, 23, 33, 35, 37, 44, 45, 47, 74, 86, 136-137
Lincoln, Abraham, 82, 179-181
Locke, John, 16, 19, 21, 23-24, 105-106, 115-117
Louis Napoleon, 54
Louis Philippe, 52, 54

MacDonald, J. Ramsay, 48
MacMahon Affair, 55
Malthus, Thomas Robert, 32, 34, 33-135
Manchester School, 41, 42, 43
Mazzini, Joseph, 61-62, 164-165
Mill, James, 41, 42
Mill, John Stuart, 44-46, 145-148
Millerand, Alexandre, 162
Milton, John, 15, 101-102
Montesquieu, 16, 24, 118-119
Mussolini, Benito, 65-66

Nationalism, 31-32, 61, 70, 81, 82, 164-165
Natural Rights, 11, 24, 29, 89, 124, 141
Nazism, *see* Fascism
Negroes, 43, 79, 82-83, 86-87, 176, 181, 185-186
New Deal, 86
Northwest Ordinance of 1787, 78, 175-176

Parties, political, 28, 43, 47, 48, 49
Philosophes, 17, 25
Philosophic Radicalism, 41, 42
Physiocrats, 22
Populism, 83
Progress, 12, 18, 103-104
Progressivism, American, 84ff
Protestant Reformation, 16

Quesnay, François, 22

Rationalism, 12, 15, 17, 100, 167
Rechtstaat, 73
Reform, parliamentary, 40-41, 42, 43, 46, 149-150; see Democracy
Reform, social, 36-37, 44, 47, 48-49, 54, 58, 65, 67, 74, 75, 85-86, 138, 141, 153-154, 174
Religion, 12, 14-15, 19-20, 105-106
Renaissance, 16
Revolution of 1830, 51; of 1848, 54, 63, 70-71
Revolution, right of, 24, 25, 116, 124-125

Ricardo, David, 32, 33, 131-132
Roman Question, 60, 64, 65, 67
Roosevelt, Franklin D., 85ff., 184-185
Roosevelt, Theodore, 84
Rousseau, Jean Jacques, 16, 18, 21, 25, 120-121
Royer-Collard, Pierre Paul, 51

Scientific Revolution, 16
Separation of Powers of Government, 118-119, 130
Slavery, 43, 79, 82, 176, 181
Smith, Adam, 16, 22-23, 33, 112-114
Socialism, 48, 54, 56-58, 59, 65, 74, 84, 152, 162-163
Socrates, 14, 94
Spencer, Herbert, 35, 136-137

Thought, freedom of, 11, 14-15, 20, 29, 45, 55, 74, 94, 98, 101, 126, 130, 141, 146-148, 169, 177-178
Tocqueville, Alexis de, 53-54, 158-159
Toleration, religious, 12, 19-20, 28, 29, 30, 40, 41, 44, 46, 105-108, 175-176
Trade unions, 38, 41, 46, 57, 65, 66, 84, 142
Troeltsch, Ernst, 171-172
Treitschke, Heinrich von, 172-173

United Nations, 38
Universal Declaration of Human Rights, 38, 139-142
Utilitarianism, 41-42

Voltaire, 16, 20, 107ff.

Weimar Republic, 75, 76
Welfare State, 37, 38, 49, 59, 67, 85, 153-154
Wilson, Woodrow, 84, 85

VAN NOSTRAND ANVIL BOOKS already published

No. 1 MAKING OF THE MODERN FRENCH MIND
By Hans Kohn
No. 2 THE AMERICAN REVOLUTION: A Short History—By Richard B. Morris
No. 3 THE LATE VICTORIANS: A Short History
By Herman Ausubel
No. 4 THE WORLD IN THE TWENTIETH CENTURY
By Louis L. Snyder
No. 5 50 MAJOR DOCUMENTS OF THE TWENTIETH CENTURY—By Louis L. Snyder
No. 6 THE AGE OF REASON—By Louis L. Snyder
No. 7 MARX AND THE MARXISTS: The Ambiguous Legacy—By Sidney Hook
No. 8 NATIONALISM: Its Meaning and History
By Hans Kohn
No. 9 MODERN JAPAN: A Brief History
By Arthur Tiedemann
No. 10 50 MAJOR DOCUMENTS OF THE NINETEENTH CENTURY—By Louis L. Snyder
No. 11 CONSERVATISM: From John Adams to Churchill
By Peter Viereck
No. 12 THE PAPACY: A Brief History
By James A. Corbett
No. 13 THE AGE OF THE REFORMATION
By Roland H. Bainton
No. 14 BASIC DOCUMENTS IN AMERICAN HISTORY
By Richard B. Morris
No. 15 CONTEMPORARY AFRICA: Continent in Transition—By T. Walter Wallbank
No. 16 THE RUSSIAN REVOLUTIONS OF 1917
By John Shelton Curtiss
No. 17 THE GREEK MIND—By Walter R. Agard
No. 18 BRITISH CONSTITUTIONAL HISTORY SINCE 1832—By Robert Livingston Schuyler and Corinne Comstock Weston
No. 19 THE NEGRO IN THE UNITED STATES: A Brief History—By Rayford W. Logan
No. 20 AMERICAN CAPITALISM: Its Promise and Accomplishment—By Louis M. Hacker
No. 21 LIBERALISM—By J. Salwyn Schapiro
No. 22 THE ERA OF THE FRENCH REVOLUTION, 1789-1799: Ten Years That Shook the World
By Leo Gershoy
No. 23 BASIC HISTORY OF MODERN GERMANY
By Louis L. Snyder
No. 24 BASIC HISTORY OF MODERN RUSSIA: Political, Cultural and Social Trends—By Hans Kohn